£2=99
6A/HS

ROLAND SCHIMMELPFENNIG

Winter Solstice

Translated by DAVID TUSHINGHAM

First performed at the Orange Tree Theatre, Richmond,
on 12 January 2017

Introduction

Roland Barthes makes the distinction between *product* and *production*, the first merely a consumer item, the second the result of an imaginative encounter between reader and text. Transposed to the theatre – where use of the word *product* is currently in terrifying ascendance – Roland Schimmelpfennig is a champion of the second method, consistently writing plays that activate and engage audiences through innovative strategies. In this play alone he co-opts cinema's use of perspective, the novel's expansive delight in language, forges a mini-opera and riffs critically on the power of music and the utility of art – including a garbled, knowing wink to Barthes put in the mouth of the inarticulate painter Konrad: "Being able to produce, you know, production, working, the work is sacred."

But the work is sacred and since we know that by engaging in production in Barthes' sense of the word, we simultaneously take up a position in relation to consumerism, there is no doubt that these plays also push us to a political position. This becomes doubly clear as the content of *Winter Solstice* comes into focus: the eternal return of the right and the seduction of fascism in its evolving forms. Written over winter 2013/14, the play now receives its English language premiere two days ahead of the inauguration of President Donald J Trump, proving the axiom that artists are often the canary in the coal-mine, better able to divine our collective futures.

This is the third Roland Schimmelpfennig play to be premiered by Actors Touring Company: Gordon Anderson directed *Arabian Night* in 2002 and I directed *The Golden Dragon* as my inaugural ATC production in 2011. This, unusually for a British theatre company, makes him, as the Germans would say, our *Hausautor*. Since we are devoted to introducing the most important international voices to the UK that may come as no surprise but as a touring company depends on the imaginative collaboration of those who run the buildings, I must record here a great debt to Paul Miller and his fantastic team at the Orange Tree who pounced on this play when many other managements passed up the chance: thank you!

In 2018, ATC will have been going for forty years. During that time countless actors, many playwrights, designers, artistic directors and their teams have tirelessly kept the idea of an open, lean, challenging and playful theatre with a cosmopolitan twist alive, sharing the work across England, the UK and the world. *Winter Solstice* is a great addition to our catalogue and one which I trust marks a continuation rather than an end.

Ramin Gray
Vienna, January 2017

KATE FAHY
Corinna

Theatre includes *Handbagged* (Tricycle tour); *After Electra* (Tricycle); *Definitely the Bahamas* (Orange Tree); *The Goat* (Almeida and Apollo, West End); *Copenhagen* (Watford); *Grace, Gaucho* and *Sparrowfall* (Hampstead Theatre); *Seduced* (Royal Court); *Old Flames* (Arts Theatre); *A Doll's House* (Riverside Studios); *Bouncing, Sunday Morning* (National Theatre); *Othello* (Young Vic); *Seduced* (Royal Court).

TV includes *The Suspicions of Mr Whicher, The Marriage of Reason and Squalor, Holby City, Death in Paradise, Cherished, Pure Wickedness, The Best Man, Poirot, Silent Witness, The House of Elliott, The Jury, Trial and Retribution, The Mozart Inquest, Danton's Death, Terra Nova, Oxbridge Blues, The Lodger, The Nearly Man.*

Film includes Joanna Hogg's *Archipelago, Defiance, Brilliance, The Show,* and *The Living and The Dead* for which she won both Best Actress (Austin) and Best Supporting Actress (Campobasso), *The Fourth Angel, Somewhere Sometime*

She directed Jean-Claude Carriere's *Little Black Book* (Park Theatre) and Oliver Cotton's *Wet Weather Cover* (King's Head Theatre and Arts Theatre, West End).

NICHOLAS LE PREVOST
Rudolph

Recent theatre includes *How the Other Half Loves* (West End); *Love for Love* and Benedick in *Much Ado About Nothing* (RSC); *Man and Superman, People* and *My Fair Lady* (National Theatre); The Rivals (Arcola); *A Marvellous Year for Plums* (Chichester); *Dandy Dick* (Theatre Royal Brighton/tour); *My Fair Lady* (Théâtre Châtelet, Paris); *27* (National Theatre of Scotland); Jonathan Harvey's opera *Wagner Dream* (Barbican); *The Philadelphia Story* (Old Vic); the title role in *Uncle Vanya* (Peter Hall Company); and *The Wild Duck* (Donmar).

TV includes *Father Brown, Above Suspicion, Cranford, Margaret, Psychoville, Wild at Heart, Half Broken Things, Life Begins, Poirot* and *The Jewel in the Crown.*

Films include *Testament of Youth, Broken Lines, Run for Your Wife, A Very British Scandal, Bright Young Things, Shakespeare in Love* and *Land Girls.*

Recent radio includes *Our Country's Good* and *HR.*

Nicholas is a founder member of The Wrestling School, a company dedicated to the work of the playwright Howard Barker.

LAURA ROGERS
Bettina

Theatre includes *A Lovely Sunday for Creve Coeur* (Print Room); Private Lives (UK tour); *Tipping the Velvet* (Lyric Hammersmith); *An Ideal Husband, Pressure, Blue Remembered Hills* and *Hay Fever* (Chichester); *Masterpieces* (Royal Court); *Three Sisters* (The Wapping Project); *55 Days, Revelations* (Hampstead); Lady Macbeth in *Macbeth, The Comedy of Errors, A New World: The Life of Thomas Paine, Timon of Athens, A Midsummer Night's Dream, The Taming of the Shrew* and *Richard III* (Shakespeare's Globe); *39 Steps* (West End); Gloucestershire (Arcola); *See How They Run* (Royal Exchange); *Bad Girls: The Musical* (West Yortkshire Playhouse/ Garrick); *The Three Musketeers* and *The Barber of Seville* (Bristol Old Vic); Celestina (BIrmingham Rep/Edinburgh International Festival/The Hague); *Jamaica Inn* (Salisbury Playhouse); *Revelations* (Hampstead); *Hay Fever* (Oxford Stage Company); and *Blackwater Angel* (Abbey).

TV includes *Holby City, New Tricks, The Smoke, Law and Order, Dates, Dark Matters, Twelfth Night, Doctor Who, Midsomer Murders, Albert's Memorial, Missing, Elvis Mania, Bad Girls, Rockface, Relic Hunter, The Sins, Tales from the Pleasure Beach* and *Running Scared.*

Films include *Love Me Do*.

Radio includes *Death of a Salesman, Porshia, Black Train* and *Someone Somewhere*.

DOMINIC ROWAN
Albert

Dominic trained at Central School of Speech and Drama.

Theatre includes *Stepping Out* (UK tour); *Giving* (Hampstead); *The Tempest, Measure for Measure, Henry VIII, A New World* and *As You Like It* (Shakespeare's Globe); *Ah, Wilderness!* and *The Cherry Orchard* (Young Vic); *Medea, Happy Now?, A Dream Play, Iphigenia at Aulis, Mourning Becomes Electra, Three Sisters, The Talking Cure* and *Private Lives* (National Theatre); *Berenice, A Voyage Round My Father* and *Lobby Hero* (Donmar); *A Doll's House* (Young Vic/West End/BAM, New York); *The Village Bike, Way to Heaven* and *Forty Winks* (Royal Court); *The Misanthrope, Under the Blue Sky* (West End); *After Dido* (ENO/Young Vic); *The Rivals, Looks Back in Anger* and *Charley's Aunt* (Royal Exchange); *A Collier's Friday Night* (Hampstead); *The Importance of Being Earnest* (Oxford Playhouse); *Sexual Perversity in Chicago* (Sheffield Crucible); *The Merchant of Venice, The Two Gentlemen of Verona* and *Talk of the City* (RSC).

TV includes *The Hollow Crown: Henry IV, Silent Witness, Restless, Law and Order UK, Catwalk Dogs, Baby Boom, Trial and Retribution, The Lavender List, The Family Man, Rescue Me, Lost World, Swallow, North Square, Hearts and Bones, A Rather English Marriage, Between the Lines, Devil's Advocate, No Bananas, Emma* and *The Tennant of Wildfell Hall*.

Films include *Tulse Luper Suitcases*.

MILO TWOMEY
Konrad

Theatre includes *Mary Poppins* (UK tour); *Twelfth Night* (Sheffield Crucible); *Much Ado About Nothing, Lady Windermere's Fan, Blithe Spirit, The Children's Hour, An Ideal Husband, Harvey* and *She Stoops to Conquer* (Royal Exchange); *Flygirl* (Unicorn); *Richard III* (Nottingham Playhouse); *Peep* (Latitude); *Dancing at Lughnasa* (Royal & Derngate); *I Heart Peterborough* (Eastern Angles/Soho); *The Surprise of Love* and *The Phoenix of Madrid* (Theatre Royal Bath); *The Last Sign of Life* (Theatre503); *No Wise Men* (Liverpool Playhouse/Peeplykus); *Brief Encounter* (Kneehigh/UK & US tours); *The Bolero* (Arcola); *Not the End of the World* (Bristol Old Vic); *The Canterbury Tales* (RSC/West End); *The Tempest* (Southark Playhouse); *Happy Yet?, La Musica Deuxieme, Danton's Death, Shakuntala* (Gate); *Three Sisters* (Nuffield Southampton/tour); *Glastonbury* (national tour); *A Place at the Table* (Pleasance/tour); *A Busy Day* (Lyric); *Macbeth* (Queens Theatre); and *Miss Julie* (Rival Productions).

TV includes *Hat Hair, X Company, Cuffs, Endeavour, Tyrant, War and Peace, Doctors, Man Down, The Guilty, Kidz Time TV, Secrets and Words, Casualty, My Spy Family, Holby City, The Golden Hour, Trial and Retribution, Battle of Britain, Dirty War, Murder City, Odysseus, Bad Girls, EastEnders, P.O.W., The Bill, The Remedy, Band of Brothers, Liverpool One, Marchioness* and *Slap!*.

Films include *Frankyn, Cool Water, Thespian X* and *The Jolly Boys Last Stand*.

ROLAND SCHIMMELPFENNIG
Writer
Roland Schimmelpfennig was born in Göttingen in 1967. After a prolonged stay in Istanbul as a journalist, he studied stage direction at the Otto-Falkenberg-School in Munich; following his studies he became assistant director at the Kammerspiele Munich from 1995 onwards he was a member of the artistic direction of the theatre.
He has been working as a freelance author since 1996. In 1998 he went to the United States for a year and there primarily worked as a translator.

Schimmelpfennig worked as dramaturg at the Schaubühne Berlin from 1999 to 2001. In the season of 2001/2002 he was author-in-residence at the Schauspielhaus in Hamburg. Since 2000 he has been commissioned to write plays for the State Theatres in Stuttgart and Hannover, the Schauspielhaus Hamburg, the Burgtheater Vienna, the Schauspielhaus Zurich, the German Theatre Berlin and international theatres in Copenhagen, Stockholm, Toronto and Tokyo. In 2010, Roland Schimmelpfennig received the Mülheim Dramatists' Prize for his play *The Golden Dragon* the world premiere of which took place at the Burgtheater in Vienna in 2009 directed by the author. In 2016, his first novel *An einem klaren, eiskalten Januarmorgen zu Beginn des 21. Jahrhunderts* (*On a clear, freezing cold January morning at the beginning of the 21st century*) was nominated for the Leipzig Book Fair Prize. Roland Schimmelpfennig lives in Berlin and Havanna.

Awards include: Else-Lasker-Schüler Award für Emerging Playwrights for *Fisch um Fisch* (1997), Schiller Memorial Award of the State of Baden-Württemberg (1998), invitation to the Mülheimer Theatertage with *Vor langer Zeit im Mai* (2000), invitation to the Mülheimer Theatertage with *Die arabische Nacht*, commisssion for the festival Frankfurter Positionen: Vorher/Nachher (2001), invitation to the Mülheimer Theatertage with *Push Up 1-3*, Nestroy Award of the city of Vienna for Best Play for *Push Up 1-3* (2002), invitation to the Mülheimer Theatertage with *Vorher/Nachher* (2003), Best Radio Play of the Year: *Für eine bessere Welt* (2004), invitation to the Mülheimer Theatertage with *Die Frau von früher* (2005), Nestroy Award of the City of Vienna for Best Play for *Besuch bei dem Vater* (2009), Else-Lasker-Schüler Award, Award of the Mülheimer Theatertage for *Der goldene Drachen* (2010).

DAVID TUSHINGHAM
Translator
David Tushingham is a dramaturg and translator. He has worked extensively as a curator for European festivals including the Wiener Festwochen, the Ruhrtriennale, Theater der Welt and the Salzburg Festival. He adapted Salman Rushdie's *Haroun and the Sea of Stories* for the National Theatre and his numerous translations include *The Golden Dragon, Arabian Night* and *Jeff Koons* (ATC), *The Woman Before, Mr Kolpert* and *Waiting Room Germany* (Royal Court), *Idomeneus* (Gate), *My Mother Medea* (Unicorn), *Innocence* and *Ant Street* (Arcola), *Nordost* (Company of Angels) and *The Bitter Tears of Petra von Kant* (Southwark Playhouse).

RAMIN GRAY
Director
Ramin has been Artistic Director of Actors Touring Company since 2010. His productions include a new version of Aeschylus' *The Suppliant Women* by David Greig (for ATC, Royal Lyceum Theatre Edinburgh and tour); *The Events* by David Greig (Traverse, Young Vic, UK and international tours 2013-6); *The Golden Dragon* by Roland Schimmelpfennig (Traverse & UK tour); *Illusions* by Ivan Viripaev; and *Martyr* by Marius von Mayenburg (co-production with Unicorn Theatre and UK tour). Previously he was Associate Director at the Royal Court Theatre where he directed Roland Schimmelpfennig's *Push Up*, Vassily Sigarev's *Ladybird*, Presnyakov Brothers' *Terrorism*, Marius von Mayenburg's *The Ugly One* and *The Stone*, Simon Stephens'

Motortown, and Mark Ravenhill's *Over There*. For the RSC he directed David Greig's *The American Pilot*. Ramin's extensive work abroad includes the Salzburg Festival, Schaubühne Berlin, Praktika Moscow, Husets Copenhagen, Schauspielhaus Wien and many more. Ramin recently directed Gerald Barry's much acclaimed opera of *The Importance of Being Earnest* for the Royal Opera at the Barbican and Lincoln Center.

LIZZIE CLACHAN
Designer

Theatre includes *Yerma* (Young Vic); *The Suppliant Women* (ATC/Royal Lyceum Theatre Edinburgh); *Three Sisters* (Theater Basel); *The Truth* (West End Menier Chocolate Factory); *Cyprus Avenue* (Royal Court/Abbey Theatre); *Macbeth, A Season in the Congo, The Soldier's Fortune* (Young Vic); *As You Like It, The Beaux Stratagem, Treasure Island, Edward II (set), Port, A Woman Killed With Kindness* (National Theatre); *Tipping the Velvet, Contains Violence, Absolute Beginners* (Lyric Hammersmith); *The Skriker* (MIF/Royal Exchange); *Carmen Disruption* (Almeida); *Fireworks, Alder & Gibb, Gastronauts, The Witness, Jumpy* (also West End), *Our Private Life, Wastwaster, Aunt Dan and Lemon, The Girlfriend Experience, On Insomnia and Midnight* (also Festival Internacional Cervantino, Guanajuato and Centro Cultural Helenico, Mexico City), *Woman and Scarecrow, Ladybird* (Royal Court); *The Forbidden Zone* (Salzburg / Berlin); *All My Sons* (Regent's Park Open Air Theatre); *A Sorrow Beyond Dreams* (Burgtheater, Vienna); *Le Vin Herbe* (Staatsoper, Berlin); *Longing, The Trial of Ubu, Tiger Country* (Hampstead); *The Rings of Saturn* (Schauspiel Cologne); *Happy Days* (Sheffield Crucible); *Far Away* (Bristol Old Vic); *Bliss* (Staatsoper, Hamburg); *Shoot/Get Treasure/Repeat* (Paines Plough); *I'll Be the Devil, Days of Significance, The American Pilot* (RSC); *The Architects, Money, Tropicana, Amato Saltone, Ether Frolics, Dance Bear Dance, The Ballad of Bobby Francois, The Tennis Show* (Shunt); *Bedtime Story, The End of the Beginning* (Union Theatre/Young Vic); *Julie, Gobbo* (National Theatre of Scotland); *Factory Girls* (Arcola); *All in the Timing* (Peepolykus); *Moonstone* (Royal Exchange, Manchester) and *Treasure Island* (West End). She co-founded Shunt in 1998.

Lizzie won Best Design at the Theatre Awards UK for *Happy Days*.

JACK KNOWLES
Lighting Designer

Jack trained at the Central School of Speech and Drama. Recent credits include: *Cleansed* (National Theatre); *Babe, the Sheep-Pig* (Polka Theatre/UK Tour); *Much Ado About Nothing* (Mercury Theatre); *A Streetcar Named Desire, Wit* (Royal Exchange); *They Drink it in the Congo, Boy, Carmen Disruption* and *Game* (Almeida); *Much Ado About Nothing* (Mercury Theatre); *Dan and Phil: The Amazing Tour is Not on Fire* (World Tour); *Watership Down* (Watermill Theatre); *The Forbidden Zone* (Salzburg Festival/ Schaubühne Berlin/Barbican Theatre); *Kenny Morgan* (Arcola); *The Massive Tragedy of Madame Bovary!* (Liverpool Everyman/Peepolykus/UK Tour); *The Haunting of Hill House* (Liverpool Playhouse); *Travelling on One Leg* and *Happy Days* (Deutsches Schauspielhaus Hamburg); *Phaedra* (Enniskillen International Beckett Festival); *The Skriker* (MIF/Royal Exchange); *2071* (Royal Court); *Hopelessly Devoted* (Paines Plough); *The Kilburn Passion* and *The Riots* (Tricycle); *Sorrow Beyond Dreams* (Burgtheater, Vienna); *Blink* (Traverse/Soho Theatre/International Tour); *Lungs* and *Yellow Wallpaper* (Schaubühne Berlin); *There Has Possibly Been An Incident* (Royal Exchange/UK Tour); *Moth* (Hightide/Bush Theatre); *The Changeling* (Young Vic, with James Farncombe); *Grounded* (Deafinitely Theatre); *Tommy* (Prince Edward Theatre); *Night Train* (Halle Kalk, Schauspiel Köln); *If That's All There Is* (International Tour); *Red Sea Fish* (59E59 New York); *In a Pickle* (RSC/Oily Cart); *Ring-A-Ding-Ding* (Unicorn Theatre/New Victory Theatre New York/Oily Cart); *Land of Lights, Light Show, There Was An Old Woman, The Bounce* and *Mr & Mrs Moon* (Oily Cart). jackknowles.co.uk

ALEXANDER CAPLEN
Sound Designer
For Actors Touring Company: *Martyr, The Events, Crave, Illusions, The Golden Dragon.*

Other Theatre Includes: *The Invisible Hand* (Tricycle); *People, Places & Things* (Associate) *We Want You to Watch, Hotel,* The Dorfman Opening Gala (National Theatre); *Red Velvet* (Associate – SAW NY Transfer); *A Time to Reap, Ding Dong the Wicked, Goodbye to All That, Wanderlust* (Royal Court); *Over There* (Royal Court & Schaubühne Berlin); *Constellations* (Associate – Duke of York's); *Donkey Heart* (Old Red Lion/Trafalgar Studios) *Ogres* (Tristan Bates); *It's About Time* (Nabokov); *Mine, Ten Tiny Toes, War and Peace* (Shared Experience); *Peter Pan, Holes, Duck Variations* (UK Tour); *The Wizard of Oz, The Entertainer* (Nuffield Theatre).

Opera includes: *The Love for Three Oranges, Tosca* (Grange Park Opera).

Alex is an Associate Artist (Sound) for ATC.

ROSEMARY McKENNA
Assistant Director
Rosemary studied at Trinity College Dublin, and trained as a director on the Rough Magic SEEDS programme. She is an Associate Director for Actors Touring Company and her work for the company includes *Martyr* at the Unicorn and on UK tour; and *The Events* at New York Theatre Workshop. As a director, her work includes *Apollonia* at the Project Arts Centre for the Dublin Theatre Festival; *Snow Angels* and *Way to Heaven* (nominated as Best Director at the Irish Times Theatre Awards) at Project Arts Centre; *Anna in Between* for the Dublin Fringe Festival; *Heroin(e) for Breakfast* at Smock Alley Theatre; *Bedbound* at the New Theatre and Samuel Beckett Theatre; and *The Importance of Being Earnest* at the Samuel Beckett Theatre. Rosemary has also worked as a Staff Director at The National Theatre on *Here We Go, The Deep Blue Sea* and *The Red Barn.* As assistant director work includes *The Critic* at Dublin Theatre Festival; *Hero* at the Royal Court; *The Housekeeper* at Project Arts Centre; and *Medea* at Samuel Beckett Theatre.

Orange Tree Theatre

t its home in Richmond, South West ondon, the Orange Tree Theatre aims to elight, challenge, move and amaze with a old and continually evolving mix of new and ediscovered plays in our unique in-the-ound space. We want to change lives by elling remarkable stories from a wide variety f times and places, filtered through the ingular imagination of our writers and the emarkable close-up presence of our actors.

Over its forty-five-year history the Orange ree has had an exceptional track record n discovering writers and promoting their arly work, as well as rediscovering artists rom the past whose work had either been isregarded or forgotten.

n the last two years, the OT has been ecognised for its work with ten major ndustry awards, including five Offies (Off Nest End Awards), three UK Theatre Awards, the Alfred Fagon Audience Award nd the Peter Brook Empty Space Award.

n 2016 the Orange Tree's work was seen in 24 other towns and cities across the country.

COMING SOON

16 FEB - 25 MAR
Low Level Panic
BY CLARE McINTYRE

17 - 25 MAR
Shakespeare Up Close
Twelfth Night

30 MAR - 13 MAY
The Lottery of Love
BY PIERRE MARIVAUX
TRANSLATED BY JOHN FOWLES

18 MAY - 24 JUN
An Octoroon
BY BRANDEN JACOBS-JENKINS

orangetreetheatre.co.uk
020 8940 3633

 OrangeTreeThtr OrangeTreeTheatre

Artistic Director **Paul Miller** Executive Director **Sarah Nicholson**

The Orange Tree is a registered charity (no. 266128) and is generously supported by the London Borough of Richmond upon Thames.

With thanks to all our Members, Patrons and funders.
Visit the website to discover how you could support the OT.

ACTORS TOURING COMPANY

Actors Touring Company makes international, contemporary theatre that travels. We create shows with a global perspective: activating and entertaining the audience whilst asking questions of the world around us. Placing the actor at the heart of our work, and employing a lean aesthetic which promotes environmental sustainability, we have toured the UK and internationally since we were founded in 1978, reaching audiences far and wide.

Recent productions include *The Suppliant Women* by Aeschylus, in a new version by David Greig, composed by John Browne and choreographed by Sasha Milavic Davies. The production launched David Greig's inaugural season as Artistic Director of the Royal Lyceum Theatre Edinburgh, who also co-produced with ATC; it then headlined the Belfast International Arts Festival at the Grand Opera House and travelled to Newcastle's Northern Stage. The production is recreated everywhere it goes, with the core company being drawn from each city's community, who rehearse for 2 months prior to their performances. Following critical and audience acclaim, *The Suppliant Women* will be revived for the Royal Exchange Theatre Manchester in 2017. Other recent work includes *Living with the Lights On* by Mark Lockyer, which toured to theatres and medical settings prior to an extended run in London in co-production with the Young Vic.

ATC's previous productions include *The Events* by David Greig, with music by John Browne, which toured extensively in the UK, the US and internationally and enjoyed revivals in Denmark, France and Australia; *The Golden Dragon* by Roland Schimmelpfennig (Traverse & UK tour); and *Martyr* by Marius Von Mayenburg (co-production with Unicorn Theatre and UK tour).

Future productions include a UK and international tour of *Living with the Lights On*; and making *The Suppliant Women* with communities in Manchester.

Artistic Director: **Ramin Gray**
Executive Director: **Andrew Smaje**
General Manager: **Jess Banks**
Chair: **Maria Delgado**
Press: **David Burns** info@davidburnspr.com 07789 754089
www.atctheatre.com

 actorstouringcompany

 ATCLondon

Supported using public funding by
**ARTS COUNCIL
ENGLAND**

ATC is a registered charity No. 279458

WINTER SOLSTICE

Roland Schimmelpfennig

WINTER SOLSTICE

OBERON BOOKS
LONDON

WWW.OBERONBOOKS.COM

First published in 2017 by Oberon Books Ltd
521 Caledonian Road, London N7 9RH
Tel: +44 (0) 20 7607 3637 / Fax: +44 (0) 20 7607 3629
e-mail: info@oberonbooks.com
www.oberonbooks.com

Originally published as: *"Wintersonnenwende"* © S. Fischer Verlag GmbH,
Frankfurt am Main, 2014

Translation copyright © David Tushingham, 2017

A catalogue record for this book is available from the British Library.

PB ISBN: 9781786820563
E ISBN: 9781786820570

Cover image design by Annie Rushton

Printed and bound by 4edge Limited, Essex, UK.
eBook conversion by CPI Group (UK) Ltd, Croydon, CR0 4YY.

Visit www.oberonbooks.com to read more about all our books and to buy
them. You will also find features, author interviews and news of any author
events, and you can sign up for e-newsletters so that you're always first to
hear about our new releases.

Characters

ALBERT

BETTINA

CORINNA

RUDOLPH

KONRAD

Marie and Naomi, both unseen.

*Lines in addition to the dialogues are spoken –
as far as possible.*

Winter Solstice opened on 18th January 2017 at the Orange Tree Theatre, London

Cast:

ALBERT	Dominic Rowan
BETTINA	Laura Rogers
CORINNA	Kate Fahy
RUDOLPH	Nicholas Le Prevost
KONRAD	Milo Twomey

Director	Ramin Gray
Designer	Lizzie Clachan
Lighting Designer	Jack Knowles
Sound Designer	Alex Caplen
Costume Supervisor	Johanna Coe
Assistant Director	Rosemary McKenna

An Orange Tree Theatre and Actors Touring Company co-production

This translation was commissioned by Actors Touring Company with the support of the Goethe-Institut London.

1.1.

ALBERT and BETTINA, both more than eager to take offense.

ALBERT
Why can't you say hello to your mother?
Why don't you just say hello to your mother?

BETTINA
I was –

ALBERT
Why is it always me who has to do it –

BETTINA
I had to – it was urgent – I had to talk to –

ALBERT
Every time she comes through the door you either run off
somewhere or you won't get off the phone –

BETTINA
I couldn't – I had the producer –

ALBERT
And I'm left standing there with her –

BETTINA
If I can't get the producer –

ALBERT
I get left standing with her, making small talk – and I hate
small talk!

1.2.

Piano music. Chopin. Nocturne No. 2.
Winter.
It's evening.
Warm light.
Outside it's night.
It's a very cold northern night,
and outside the large windows
it's snowing.
Titles.

1.3.

ALBERT
Why can't you just say hello to her?

7

BETTINA
I couldn't – say hello –

ALBERT
You don't say anything to her and leave me standing there
with her –

BETTINA
The producer was more important, you wouldn't make your
editor –

1.4.

Producer.
He hates that word. And he knows it wasn't the producer she
was talking to, it was someone else.
His angry face.
Her angry face.
Outside snow falls through circles of light cast by the city
streetlamps.
They argue but they argue
in hushed voices, so her mother won't hear them
or their daughter either.

1.5.

BETTINA
The producer was more important, you wouldn't make your
editor –

ALBERT
What do you mean: more important? You always do this. Do
you think she doesn't notice, do you think I don't notice, do
you think Marie doesn't notice?

BETTINA
Oh come on – if you –

ALBERT
And it's like this every time, every time –

BETTINA
What's it got to do with you –

ALBERT
I'm not doing this any more.
No, that's it, I'm not doing this any more – that was the last
time –

BETTINA
You know something?

ALBERT
What?

BETTINA
Go fuck yourself.

1.6

A wealthy, middle class living room in our time.
An old building. Europe.
The people who live here have taste, they skilfully combine
old and modern, they have plenty of money but things don't
have to be perfect.
Ikea meets Biedermeier and Charles Eames and the flea
market.
They read books, they have gone to university.

1.7.

BETTINA
Go fuck yourself. Just keep out of it –

ALBERT
Keep out of it – how am I supposed to keep out of it – I'm the
one standing there in the corridor with her, me, not you, *you're*
on the phone. It's a matter of politeness, a matter of respect –

1.8.

High ceilings, double doors.
A lot of space.
A lot of books.
An old piano.
The people who live here have never voted for a conservative
party in their lives. They are no older than mid-forties, but
could be younger. Perhaps they're still in their late thirties.
They've arrived where they wanted to get to.
On one wall there's a large oil painting, the work of a friend.
A large, expressive work. It's hard to tell what the work
represents. Several human bodies perhaps.
Pain.
Desire.
Dependence.
Injuries.

1.9.

ALBERT
It's a matter of politeness, it's a matter of respect –

1.10.

Politeness and respect:
Bettina's eyes narrow with anger at these words.
Bettina and Albert have an eight-year-old child, a girl, Marie.

1.11.

BETTINA
My mother and I left all manner of politeness and all manner of respect behind us a long time ago – don't you worry about that.

1.12.

All manner. She says "all manner".
He, Albert, is a publisher, sociologist, historian and a respected essayist. Sometimes he writes fiction, short stories. He's the classic intellectual: casual, careless, with glasses, seeming to lack vanity but vain at the same time.
Bettina is slim, good-looking, creative, highly intelligent, an elegant woman, even if this evening she's just wearing a pair of jeans and a white t-shirt – Bettina has many talents, perhaps too many: she has worked as a writer, a dancer, a stage designer, an illustrator, but now she's doing what she has really wanted to do for years: she directs her own films. These are clever, sometimes uncomfortable and unusual films which are therefore difficult to market, not for mass audiences.

1.13.

BETTINA
But what's it even got to do with you? What's it got to do with you? –

ALBERT
It's to do with me when you go creeping off –

1.14.

The – ee – in creep sounds as if his voice is slipping away from him.

1.15

BETTINA
Creeping off? It was an important call – they want to change
the script, they say it's too –

1.16.

There's always somebody who wants to change the script, a
producer, an editor.
It's lacking aggression, the producer said.
Make it more like the end of the world, the producer said.

1.17.

BETTINA
They want to change the script, they say it's too –

ALBERT
It has to do with me when you go and leave me alone with
her –

BETTINA
And if I haven't done it by – I –

ALBERT
Yes but not by today –

BETTINA
By today – I'm right up against it here –

1.18.

I, I, I, all she ever says is I, Albert thinks.

1.19.

ALBERT
Or should I just not open the door?
Or should I open the door when she rings the bell – unlike
you – and then leave her standing alone out on the stairs. How
humiliating –

1.20.

At the same time in the bathroom.
In the mirror, the face of a woman: in her mid-sixties or
maybe older – Bettina's mother, Corinna. An impressive
vision, a strong woman, the Nordic type.
She is putting on lipstick.

1.21.

At the same time in the living room.

ALBERT
How humiliating –

1.22.

Corinna comes to visit two or three times a year.
She comes by train from another city.
Usually the mood between mother and daughter is very tense
at the beginning of these visits. It is then alleviated with the
help of good and expensive wine but later, by the third day at
the latest, there is an argument. Today is day one, Corinna has
just arrived.
It is 6.15 pm.

1.23.

BETTINA
I'm up against it here, right up against it and if I haven't got it
done by January –

ALBERT
I could do that. I could just leave her standing in the corridor
but you know what would happen then. You don't do things
like that, I don't do things like that, for Marie's sake too, she is
her grandmother after all –

BETTINA
By January – and today's the –

1.24.

If Bettina hasn't started filming by January or February at the
very latest, the film is dead because the film is set in winter. It's
a winter film.

1.25.

ALBERT
Marie is happy –

1.26.

The warm light of the living room.
Outside more snow is falling and snow will continue to fall all
night.
There is nobody out there.

It is Saturday 24th December. Tomorrow is Christmas Day.

1.27.

ALBERT
She's happy, as you might imagine, she's only got one
grandmother –

1.28.

Bettina looks past Albert at the books on the shelves behind
him. The books that he has written in the last twenty years.
One every couple of years, sometimes two.
The titles of some of his books:
'Extermination', 'The Future of the Past',
'An Incomplete History of Human Experiments',
'Dictatorship and Death'
'Human Dignity' and his first collection of short stories:
'When We Loved Each Other'.
Next to them on the shelf: A lot of books by other authors on
the Third Reich, on fascism, anti-Semitism and the Holocaust.

1.29.

ALBERT
She's happy, as you might imagine, she's only got one
grandmother – and you leave her standing outside. Having a
grandmother is something special –

1.30.

In recent years she's stopped reading his books. But she knows
what's in them or she thinks she knows.

1.31.

ALBERT
So Marie should at least have some contact with her one
grandmother – and we should at least let the woman in –

1.32.

Albert's mother died five years ago in France, in a swimming
accident on the Atlantic coast.
His father committed suicide when Albert was still a child.

2.1.

CORINNA
Bettina!

2.2.

The grandmother shouts from the bathroom.
A rough voice. A powerful voice. One feels one can hear her
entire life, which has not been an easy one.
Cigarettes. Alcohol. A voice which shifts between accusation
and self-defence, self-assurance, inadequacy, enthusiasm and
fear.

2.3.

CORINNA from the bathroom.
Bettina?
Bettina?

BETTINA
Yes –

CORINNA
Haven't you got any soap?

ALBERT quietly.
Haven't we got any soap?
We have got soap.

BETTINA loud.
We've got soap. It's where the soap always is.

To Albert: Have you asked her how long she's staying?

ALBERT
How, why, how am I supposed to do that?

BETTINA
Ask, it's quite simple –

ALBERT
You ask her –

BETTINA
I can't ask her –

ALBERT
Neither can I. She's your mother, and it's Christmas –

BETTINA
And she didn't say anything?

ALBERT
No –

BETTINA
What?

ALBERT
No –

BETTINA
So she did say something.
She *said* something.

ALBERT
She asked what our plans are for Marie's birthday.

2.4.

Albert should have told Bettina straight away – but he didn't.

2.5.

BETTINA
So she's staying till Marie's birthday.

ALBERT
But that's not for a fortnight.

BETTINA
And it means we'll have her in the house on New Year's Eve.
Like last year. Just like last year.

ALBERT
But that's not –

BETTINA
You wanted it that way –

ALBERT
We've got people coming on New Year's Eve. Guests. Friends.
You know how she offended those people. Last year.

2.6

"Editor – isn't that supposed to be something edible?"
Corinna had said to his editor, last year, when she was drunk.

2.7.

ALBERT
She offends people, especially people she doesn't know and
who are important. Especially women. Especially women who
are younger than her, and these women's partners – basically
everyone –

BETTINA
Because you didn't ask her.

ALBERT
What?

BETTINA
Because you're too much of a coward.

ALBERT
Excuse me, I am not a coward.

BETTINA
You can't stand conflict –

ALBERT
I opened the door to her. It's Christmas. YOU invited her. YOU invited her several times on the phone –

BETTINA
I'd been drinking –

ALBERT
You get drunk and then you get sentimental, and then you invite her without making it clear how long –

BETTINA
You can't make it clear, if you set a limit, she feels unwelcome –

ALBERT
She's just had a six hour train journey. Her train got stuck in the middle of nowhere, in the snow, and then the heating failed –

BETTINA
Of course –

ALBERT
She arrives here half frozen and I'm supposed to chuck her out before she's unpacked her suitcase –

BETTINA
Why can't you open your mouth –
Why can't you just open your mouth for once –

2.8.

CORINNA shouts from the depths of the apartment.

Bettina?!

2.9.

Something smashes somewhere at the back of the large apartment. A noise like a glass being dropped. A look between the two of them.

2.10.

BETTINA shouts.
What was that?

BETTINA shouts again.
What was that?

2.11.

No answer.
It is 6.20 p.m.

2.12.

BETTINA
You didn't even say anything when our daughter fell through the ice when she went skating.

ALBERT
No one fell through the ice –

BETTINA
First she offends our guests and then she practically kills our daughter –

ALBERT
She's your mother, not mine.

BETTINA
This is your family. Do you want your daughter and I to be spending Christmas, New Year's Eve and her birthday with that woman?

ALBERT
That woman –

BETTINA
Is that what you want? Yes, you do want that! Why do you keep going behind my back? Why don't you defend me? No, it's worse, I can defend myself, but why don't you defend yourself? Why don't you defend our child?

2.13.

> Outside it doesn't stop snowing.
> They should start preparing something to eat.
> They've got to decorate the Christmas tree
> because as in previous years
> there won't be enough time tomorrow –
> but the tree is still downstairs in the car.

2.14.

ALBERT

I do defend myself – I just have a different way of dealing with these things –

BETTINA

You don't have any way of dealing with them. The only way you have is a way of avoiding them.

2.15.

> The doorbell rings. It is an old fashioned, wealthy, middle class doorbell.

3.1.

ALBERT
Who is it?
Who is it?

BETTINA
No idea.

ALBERT shouts:
Can you open it, Marie?
Marie, can you hear me,
Can you open it?

3.2.

> Marie is their child.
> She always runs to the door when the bell rings.
> Like a dog, Bettina thinks every time. Like a dog – and Bettina wonders whether this is a cruel thought or a loving one.
> For a moment there is silence.
> Then Marie shouts: Nooo! I can't – I'm in the bathroom with Grandmaaa – she's got a new dreeess –
> Her grandmother's voice: Well you are a one, that was supposed to be a surprise –

The doorbell rings again.

3.3.

ALBERT
Are you expecting anybody?

BETTINA
It could be the postman –

ALBERT
The postman? At this time?

BETTINA
Or Konrad –

ALBERT
Marie, please open the door!
Maybe Father Christmas got the day wrong.

3.4.

The child shouts cheerfully: All riiight.
She runs out of the bathroom along the corridor to the
entrance hall. Light, exuberant, happy child steps.
The little girl is pulling something along the corridor behind
her, a piece of string with something tied onto it, an old
toothbrush that rattles across the floorboards. Her horse – she
calls it her horse. Come on, come on, horsey! the girl shouts.

3.5.

BETTINA
Konrad said he might pop in later –

3.6.

Konrad. Konrad is the painter who painted the large
expressive picture. A friend of the family. Konrad and Albert
have been friends since they were children.
The girl shouts excitedly and cheerfully from the hallway:
Daddy! Daddy!
We've got a visitor!
Albert is pleased she is so excited. To the girl, everything is
special.
Her grandmother's visit.
Christmas tomorrow. And in a fortnight she will be eight. He
shouts:

3.7.

ALBERT
What? Who is it? Who's there?

3.8.

The girl running. The toothbrush on a string clattering.
Her horse.
Like a dog, her mother thinks.
The child shouts as she goes:
A visiitoor! A visiitoor! I don't know who!
Doors slamming.
Albert takes a step backwards towards the double doors which
lead from the living room to the entrance hall.

3.9.

ALBERT
Yes but who is it? Who's come, Marie?

3.10.1.

Marie further off in the depths of the apartment.
"Grandma, Grandma, we've got a visitor."

3.10.2.

CORINNA in a rather too cheery, slightly drunken voice:
Whaaat?

3.11.

Bettina knows her mother's voice.
She can hear when her mother is lying, she can hear it straight
away, and her mother lies a lot, but why should her mother be
lying now –

3.12.

CORINNA
Really? A visitor? Now? Who on earth can that be?

3.13.

Albert turns to go to the front door.
Someone is already standing between the large, half open
double doors into the living room – a slim, good-looking man
with a charming smile. The man knocks carefully four times
on the frame of the door.
Knock knock knock knock.

3.14.

Albert is startled.
Who are you?

3.15.

The man is perhaps in his mid-sixties or even a little older.
He wears a grey suit and a heavy overcoat. He has an old
suitcase, perhaps a hat too.
He creates the slight impression of coming from another time.

3.16.

RUDOLPH smiles regretfully –
Excuse me – Excuse me for just walking in here – but the
child –

3.17.

The man smiles and gestures towards the front door –

3.18.

RUDOLPH rather awkward, explaining himself.
The child opened the door, and then the light on the stairs
went out, what a splendid, beautiful staircase, wonderful these
old buildings, and I couldn't find the light switch, so I was
standing there in the dark and I didn't want you not to be able
to see me when you –

BETTINA
What –

RUDOLPH
My name is Rudolph –

3.19.

The man just beyond the large, white double doors looks as
if he has had a long journey. He is holding a small piece of
paper which he twists nervously between his fingers. The man
finds the situation rather uncomfortable. This is clearly not the
reception he had anticipated.

3.20.

RUDOLPH
You must excuse me, I'm looking for –

3.21.

From the depths of the apartment Bettina's mother shouts:

CORINNA
Bettina! Haven't you got any towels?

3.22.

It's not the first time she's been here. She knows where the towels are kept.

3.23.

BETTINA shouts.
Yes, Mother, we *do* have towels. Just have a look and you'll find them.

3.24.

A trace of relief in the stranger's face which Albert spots without knowing what it means yet –

3.25.

RUDOLPH
I – I was – I'm looking for – She gave me this address – she invited me –
I'd like to see Gudrun.

ALBERT
Who?

RUDOLPH
Gudrun?

ALBERT
Gudrun – what Gudrun –

RUDOLPH
She, she gave me this address – This is the right place, isn't it –

ALBERT
There's no Gudrun living here –

BETTINA
He wants to see my mother.
You want to see my mother –

ALBERT
But your mother's not called Gudrun.

BETTINA
Yes she is –

ALBERT
Corinna? Corinna's called Gudrun?

BETTINA
Her middle name is Gudrun –

ALBERT
Gudrun –

RUDOLPH
Is she here?

BETTINA shouts.
Mother – Mother, you have a visitor.

3.26.

At that moment, when Bettina shouts "Mother" her voice
sounds rough and hard, similar to her mother's voice.

3.27.

RUDOLPH
She invited me –

ALBERT
Invited you?

RUDOLPH
My name is Rudolph. Rudolph Mayer. But call me Rudolph.
Pleased to meet you –

BETTINA to Albert
She said nothing to me –

ALBERT
When did she have the chance –

BETTINA
Why –

3.28.

Albert offers Rudolph his hand. An uncertain handshake.

3.29.

ALBERT
I'm Albert –

23

RUDOLPH
I – I can tell I've come at an inconvenient time, I'll be on my way –
I just wanted, because I did promise –

ALBERT
No, no, – only I, we didn't know that –

RUDOLPH apologizing.
Perhaps if I could just quickly –

3.30.

Albert looks at Bettina. Bettina shrugs her shoulders.
Why doesn't she do anything, thinks Albert.

3.31.1.

ALBERT
Corinna?!

3.31.2.

No answer.

3.31.3.

ALBERT
You must excuse us, we weren't expecting you –
Corinna?

CORINNA shouts from the depths of the apartment.
Yees??
I'm in the bathroom.

ALBERT
There's a visitor here to see you.
You've got a visitor!

CORINNA
A visitor? For me? Really?

3.32.

Bettina thinks: that tone of voice –

3.33.

CORINNA
Really? Who on earth can that be – I'll be right there.

3.34.1.

They all wait. Albert would like to say something but he
doesn't know what –

3.34.2.

ALBERT
Well –

3.35.1.

Corinna comes hastily into the living room. Corinna has
changed her clothes and put on make-up.
She sees Rudolph.

3.35.2.

CORINNA
Oh! Oh! What a surprise!
How lovely! How lovely of you to come!

3.36.

It is 6.27 p.m.

4.1.

BETTINA
How do you know this man?

CORINNA
Know him –

4.2.

6.38 p.m., ten minutes later, in the kitchen.
Bettina and Corinna.
It is a very large kitchen/dining room. A heavy dining table
ten feet long.

CORINNA
Know him, well, I don't really know him at all –

4.3.

Corinna wants to underplay the whole thing. She knows her
daughter is going to criticise her.

4.4.

BETTINA
You don't know him. But you invited him –

CORINNA
Yes, yes, of course I invited him – he said he was –

4.5.

Corinna is in urgent need of a drink.
She repeatedly places the four empty wine glasses on the table
and then picks them back up again.
The table: when Albert and Bettina first saw it in a furniture
shop fifteen years ago, they couldn't afford it but over
the following years they began to earn some money and
eventually Albert bought it. Light wood.
A very beautiful lamp over the table, actually an old hanging
lantern.
The kitchen cupboards are partly modern and partly old, a
successfully improvised combination like in the living room.
Rustic cupboards and designer items. The child's drawings on
the cupboards.
Photos. Lists. A timetable.
A large fridge with magnets stuck to it.
Magnetic sushi pieces.
Magnetic words which you can use to make sentences. Marie
sometimes plays with them.
Albert and Bettina haven't made a sentence with these
magnets for a long time.

4.6.

BETTINA
How?

CORINNA
How what?

BETTINA
How do you know him –

4.7.

Why does she always have to force me into a corner? Why
can't she just leave me alone, Corinna thinks. She thinks:
What did I do to her?
Bettina sees her mother's new dress. The dress was expensive
and later her mother will complain as she always does about
not having any money. It occurs to Bettina that the dress
is a colour called petrol. She remembers how Konrad, her
husband's best and oldest friend, wanted to explain the shades

of blue to her, the names of the different colours, in his studio
one afternoon a few weeks ago and that she'd said: let's not
talk about colours.

4.8.

CORINNA
We sat opposite each other.

BETTINA
Where?

CORINNA
On the train.

4.9.

Rather conspiratorial, rather carried away.
Rather excited, rather immature. Corinna speaks as if she has
done something forbidden. As if she is sharing a secret. In
this way she's trying to make her daughter smile, and Bettina
knows this but it's too early to give in.
Her mother inviting a stranger is an imposition, it's one of the
impositions she knows only too well.

4.10.

CORINNA
On the train.

BETTINA impatient.
On the train, on the train – on what train?

CORINNA
On the train this afternoon.

BETTINA
Oh – you met him this afternoon –

CORINNA
Yes –

BETTINA
You've invited someone you met on the train. I can't believe
it.
Today's Christmas!

CORINNA
Tomorrow, tomorrow is Christmas. And he had nowhere to

go – there were no more trains, none – because of the snow – there's absolutely nothing.

4.11.

Now she starts just slightly twisting things, dramatizing them: it's not Christmas today, it's tomorrow. The mother feels her daughter's rejection in every word. If it was up to her daughter, Corinna thinks, she could just as well die of starvation and thirst.

4.12.

CORINNA
He's got nobody –
Like me.

4.13.

There it is: her tendency towards self-pity and veiled criticism. The bitter lines around her mouth.
On the other hand: it's true. Corinna is lonely. She had hoped to be more involved in the family when Marie was born.
Of course she knows that her daughter avoids her.
And if she was being honest with herself, she'd have to admit that she also avoids her daughter – and her husband too, whom she admires but at the same time finds ridiculously unmanly. The type of man who would previously have been called "wet". Or a "wimp", she thinks.
Every time she leaves here she is both very happy and very sad. But she's also happy every time she arrives, even though this joy immediately turns into uncertainty and anger when her daughter doesn't even say hello to her because – as always – she has to make some supposedly important telephone call.

4.14.

BETTINA
In other words you have no idea who he is –

CORINNA
Yes, yes I do, we did talk to each other.
And then the train got stuck in the snow and the heating went off because the engine broke down, and then he offered me his coat, a beautiful old long heavy coat like they used to have and I liked that and I said "how chivalrous". And then he looked at me and said: "'Chivalrous', I haven't heard that word for a long time," and I said: "I haven't used it for a very

long time." And then we talked about chivalry and about
Tristan and Isolde and then we got on to Wagner, and then
he said there are so many words one doesn't hear any more.
"Decent," for example. Or "decency". Or "finesse".

4.15.

Now the daughter smiles. She smiles at how her mother
describes the encounter in the train. She thinks: a shame that
this woman doesn't make more of her life. Hasn't made more
of it. Why didn't she?
It is 6.43 p.m.

5.1.

6.54 p.m.
Albert and Bettina are alone for a moment in the kitchen.

5.2.

ALBERT
Someone she met on the train? She's invited someone she met
on the train?

5.3.

Albert with a wine bottle and corkscrew in one hand and a
packet of pills in the other.
Albert feels pressure, a tension in his stomach and in his chest,
pain in his head. He wears reading glasses.
He is visibly agitated but speaks in a hushed voice. His
mother-in-law and his daughter can be heard laughing in the
living room. Indistinct voices. His mother-in-law says: Really?
Is that really true? Rudolph answers good naturedly: Oh yes!
Anything's possible in Paraguay.
Corinna: In Paraguay – Marie: Where is this Paraguay then?
Rudolph: Far, far away from here, at the other end of the
world –
Marie: Oh –

5.4.

ALBERT
Someone she met on the train –

BETTINA
Yes.

5.5.1.

In the living room. Corinna's big eyes, her smile.

5.5.2.

CORINNA
Really? Is that really true?

RUDOLPH
Oh yes! Anything's possible in Paraguay.

CORINNA
In Paraguay –

5.6.

Paraguay – Corinna loves the sound of this word.

5.7.

In the kitchen. Albert and Bettina.

BETTINA
Typical –

ALBERT
What?

5.8.

In Albert's hand the still unopened wine bottle and the packet of pills. He puts his reading glasses on and takes them off again.

5.9.

ALBERT
What? What's typical –

BETTINA
Typical of you to apologize.

5.10.1.

In the living room. Corinna and Rudolph chat excitedly. The child sits with them, listening with big ears. She likes this strange man.

5.10.2.

CORINNA
In Paraguay.

5.11.

The sound of that word. The sound of far away. The sound of the big wide world.

5.12.

RUDOLPH
Yes, in Paraguay of all places. Argentina. Chile.

CORINNA
But are you a Paraguayan?

RUDOLPH
A Paraguayan – No, do I look like one?

5.13.

Laughter.
The child asks: So what do Paraguayans look like?

5.14.

RUDOLPH
They're really tiny. Like dwarves.

5.15.

Big child eyes.

5.16.

CORINNA
No, no, no, Rudolph, I don't believe that!

5.17.

Albert and Bettina in the kitchen.

ALBERT
What for? What did I apologize for?

BETTINA
I'll tell you what for – my mother invites someone here without saying a word to us and you, you apologize – you've no need to apologize and now you're pretending you don't know what I'm talking about–

5.18.

RUDOLPH
And they've got tiny fingers, tiny eyes – and tiny feet!

CORINNA acts outraged.
Well really!

5.19.

The child asks: really?

5.20.

CORINNA
No!

RUDOLPH
But almost.

5.21.

In the kitchen.

ALBERT
Who did I apologize to –

BETTINA
To him –

ALBERT
I'm polite.

BETTINA
You're a coward.

5.22.

The word "coward". That word wounds him – how could it
not – the word hurts. He can't remember exactly when she
first called him a "coward".
It's a word she rarely uses, but this is already the second time
it's been heard today. She uses it most when her mother is
here.
When she first started using it a couple of years ago it
sounded different, it sounded more like a joke, an affectionate
provocation perhaps, not like a definitive judgement.

5.23.

ALBERT
I'm polite.

BETTINA denigrating, his mocking echo.
Polite.

5.24.1.

Albert tries to read the information sheet for his medication.
He takes his reading glasses off, puts them back on again,
takes them off again and then puts them on but he cannot
make out the tiny print.

5.24.2.

ALBERT
How long is he going to stay – you can't simply invite yourself
–

BETTINA
He didn't invite himself. She invited him. You asked him in –

5.24.3.

The tension in his chest increases.

5.24.4.

ALBERT
I did what? I didn't do anything – he was in our house and
said he was a guest of your mother – and as usual you didn't
say a word –

5.25.

Albert takes two tablets out of the packet and holds them in
his hand.

5.26.

BETTINA
And in a minute you'll apologize that we've got nothing to eat
in the house –
I know you –

ALBERT
You didn't shop. You said you would do the shopping.

5.27.

In the living room

CORINNA cheerfully laughs out loud.
What a beautiful story!

RUDOLPH
On a mountain of crystal. Fruit everywhere – blood as pure as spring water. Living for a thousand years.

5.28.

In the kitchen.

BETTINA
How many different pills do you actually take in a day?

5.29.

Bettina takes the information sheet for the medication out of Albert's hand and skims through it. He turns the tap on.

5.30.

BETTINA
Did you read this about side effects – it says here you mustn't drink alcohol if you're taking these –
Who knows who he is.
Who knows who you've gone and let in here.

5.31.

She goes into the living room.
The producer had said:
Cinema is about the end of the world.
Cinema is about saving the world.
Albert is left standing alone in the kitchen. The water is still running. He turns the tap off.
He pours himself a glass of wine and swallows the pills.
He looks at the magnets on the fridge door: words and letters.
Marie, his daughter, has made a sentence out of them.
THE FIRE FALLS SOFTLY.
THE SNOW IS BLUE.
Almost a haiku, he thinks.
He takes his glasses off. A moment of exhaustion.
His eyesight gets worse and worse, especially in winter.
He puts a couple of the magnet words together next to Marie's sentences.
He writes:
THE NIGHT IS GOING BLIND.
Piano music.

6.1.

7.15 p.m.
Rudolph at the piano.

He is playing Chopin's Nocturne no. 2 in E minor. He plays
very, very well.
The music.
The faces.
The large oil painting.
The living room. The books.
Albert, Bettina, Corinna and Rudolph with full wine glasses.
The child, Marie, listens and plays with her toothbrush on a
string. She sits at her mother's feet.
Corinna is rapt. The child is amazed.
Bettina thinks: this would be good music for a film. This
would be wonderful music for the beginning of a film. Albert
suddenly feels hot.
Rudolph's fingers on the keyboard.
Chopin.

6.2.

In the kitchen. Some time later, around 7.30 p.m. Bettina and
Albert alone for a moment.
Albert with supressed panic.
Something's not right about this man–
And your mother's behaving like a seventeen year old.

6.3.

Music. A little earlier, 7.17 p.m. In the living room.
Rudolph at the piano.
His fingers. His half-closed eyes.
Corinna's face.
The child playing quietly.
Albert's face. He feels hot.
Bettina looking off into the distance.
On a small occasional table are some of her films on DVD.
The titles of her films:
'Robert and I'
'One Week in Germany'
'Life would not be Life.'

6.4.1.

The music continues.

6.4.2.

A woman and a man in a studio.
Large windows. Rain.

Paint, brushes, canvases, half-finished pictures, mess. He is wearing overalls. She is wearing an elegant suit.
The man is smiling and holding something behind his back. She looks at him smiling.

6.5.1.

Rudolph keeps playing.
Chopin.
Bettina, lost in thought, runs her fingers through her hair.
For a moment Albert has the feeling that he can't breathe. He wants to leave the room.
Rudolph plays the final bars of the piece, then closes the lid of the piano reverentially. The piano is a valuable heirloom, a Grotrian. Albert's father used to play this piano.
Corinna claps with delight and tries to make eye contact with her daughter.

6.5.2.

CORINNA
How beautiful! Bravo.

6.5.3.

Corinna and Marie clap.

6.6.

In the kitchen. Some time later.

ALBERT
This man's driving me mad.

BETTINA
Yes, but my mother likes him –

ALBERT
He talks intolerable rubbish –

6.7.1.

CORINNA
How beautiful! Bravo.

6.7.2.

Corinna and Marie clap.

6.7.3.

RUDOLPH modest.
It's been ages since I –

6.8.1.

He pauses.
A moment of silence follows.
Bettina knows that Albert won't be able to tolerate this
moment of embarrassment for long.
Albert hates moments like this. He hates any form of small
talk but he can't help himself, he feels he has to say something.
He takes a gulp of red wine and before he's swallowed it
properly:

6.8.2.

ALBERT
So – you met on the train.

RUDOLPH
Yes, today – the train got stuck – it literally did get stuck.

6.9.

What is there to talk about? Bettina decides to say nothing.
An ancient, almost life-long anger rises within her. She has the
feeling of being an intruder in her own living room, intruding
on her mother, just like she's felt all her life that she's been
intruding on her mother.

6.10.

ALBERT
I'm – I'm afraid we don't have very much food in the house,
we didn't realise –

6.11.

The look on Bettina's face.
Bettina laughs, bitter and amused. It's at moments like this
when Albert hates his wife.
She's laughing because she despises him. Because she hates
him for something she used to love him for – his softness,
which she now calls cowardice.

6.12.

CORINNA
Play some more!

6.13.

Rudolph smiles, rather embarrassed. He starts another piece,
a piece by Johann Sebastian Bach, the Fugue no. 17 in A-flat
major from The Well-Tempered Clavier, Book 1, BWV 862.
But then he doesn't play any further, instead he says:

6.14.

RUDOLPH
If the universe is nothing but chaos,
then how can music exist?
If the universe were nothing more than a coincidence, nothing
but disorder,
music would not exist. But it does exist
and that is proof –
that there is perfection –

6.15.1.

He starts the Bach fugue again.

6.15.2.

RUDOLPH
Listen – that is perfection –
music as order,
how wonderful, music *is* order.
The world order.

6.16.

In the kitchen, some time later. Bettina and Albert alone.

ALBERT
Did you hear that, did you hear what he said about world
order –

6.17.1.

Earlier. In the living room.

CORINNA to Albert
Didn't you write a book about that?

6.17.2.

Albert smiles awkwardly and says nothing.

6.17.3.

BETTINA
He wrote a book about music and fascism.

CORINNA
Oh, yes –

RUDOLPH
Music is –

6.18.

Rudolph is trying to find the right words –
He plays a couple of bars again. He starts with Chopin's
Nocturne –

6.19.

RUDOLPH
This is Chopin –
Chopin was Polish –
Polish – who would have thought –

6.20.1.

Albert briefly wonders: What does he mean by that? Why is
he saying that?

6.20.2.

RUDOLPH, as if he has guessed this thought:

RUDOLPH
And there aren't many Polish composers.

6.21.

Rudolph begins playing the Bach piece again.

6.22.

RUDOLPH
And this is Bach.
To say nothing of Wagner.

6.23.

He plays a Wagnerian chord.

6.24.

> RUDOLPH
> That is Wagner.

6.25.

> RUDOLPH laughs with pleasure.

6.26.

> Downfall, the producer had said.
> Pain. Hope and destruction.

6.27.

> RUDOLPH laughs with pleasure.

6.28.

> RUDOLPH
> But what would music be without the people who hear it.
> What would all this cosmic order be without the people who
> see it –
> Nothing –
>
> CORINNA
> Yes –

6.29.

> She's never thought about this.

6.30.

> RUDOLPH
> What would chaos, the universe, be without the people who
> composed this music who created this order – out of nothing –
> If I'd been a composer –

6.31.

> It's as if Rudolph were putting himself and his life on trial –

6.32.

> RUDOLPH
> If, if, if, but you're not –

6.33.

> Rudolph takes a breath, Corinna looks at Rudolph. This man
> talks so inspiringly, he is witty, he is original.

6.34.

RUDOLPH
If, if, if, but you're not –

CORINNA
So what are you then?

RUDOLPH
I – I'm a doctor –

CORINNA
A doctor – There's nothing more beautiful than saving a
human life, or many of them –

RUDOLPH
Yes, that's true.

6.35.

Rudolph gets going again.

6.36.

RUDOLPH
Mankind – yes – mankind.
Mankind is the highest.
Mankind rules the world.
Alright – not everybody. Not everyone.

6.37.

Corinna laughs. Her mouth. Her eyes.
An ageing but still beautiful woman. Simultaneously full of joy
and bitterness.
A life full of compromises, full of subservience – but she has
made the best of it.

6.38.

RUDOLPH
Everyone has their place. Don't they?

6.39.

Albert smiles awkwardly.

6.40.

RUDOLPH
One must know one's place. Like in an orchestra. Everyone
has their place. Not everyone is the composer. Not everyone is
the conductor. It's Latin. Con-duce: the leader.

6.41.

Albert does not know what to say.
The pressure in his stomach. The pressure in his chest. Albert
knows this pressure. It could be the beginning of a seizure. No
doctor has yet been able to find out where it comes from.
Where are the pills he just had – the new pills?
They're in the kitchen by the sink next to the fridge.
He drinks some red wine. He notices that the bottle is almost
empty.

6.42.

CORINNA
My place for example –

6.43.

Corinna smiles at the little girl.

6.44.

CORINNA
My place for example, our place –

6.45.

She nods to Rudolph.

6.46.

CORINNA
My place for example, our place, for example,
is now Marie's room. Show us your room.
Do you want to?

6.47.

She's saying "us".
Bettina doesn't like her mother allowing a strange man into
her daughter's room but on the other hand she is glad she
doesn't have to look after her.

6.48.

RUDOLPH
Oh. Oh yes. I stand with my troops at the ready.

6.49.

He clicks his heels together and salutes.
The grandmother laughs.
The child jumps up excitedly, clicks her heels together and salutes.
It's around 7.30 p.m.
Corinna and Rudolph leave with the little girl. The child takes the stranger's hand. Rudolph turns around and waves to Albert and Bettina.

7.1.

7.45 p.m.
In the bathroom. Albert alone.
In his hand the new pills.
He opens a mirrored cabinet. A lot of medicines. He looks for a packet and finds it. He tries to read the information leaflet. He wonders whether he can combine the old medication with the new medication but he can't read the directions. He puts his reading glasses on. He takes his reading glasses off. He holds the new tablets up next to the old ones. The old ones are white. The new ones are blue.
Music cue: Johann Sebastian Bach: Well-Tempered Clavier, Book 1, Prelude and Fugue 24 in B minor, BWV 869.
Albert ought to phone his doctor but it is Saturday. And it's Christmas. No one can be reached. He sits down on the edge of the bath. Piano music from the living room.

7.2.

At the same time in the living room. Rudolph and Corinna alone, they sit next to each other at the piano.
Rudolph plays the Prelude and Fugue 24 in B minor, BMV 869, from The Well-Tempered Clavier.
Corinna wonders whether Rudolph will try to touch her. She would like him to, but tries not to make it too obvious. She smiles. He plays the piece through to the end.
A moment of silence. Both with wine glasses in their hands.

7.3.

RUDOLPH
It's so lovely the way the little girl is so happy.

CORINNA
She likes you.

RUDOLPH
All excited –

CORINNA
Of course.
It's Christmas tomorrow.

RUDOLPH
The bright eyes of a child. Red cheeks. A healthy girl.

7.4.

In the kitchen. Albert and Bettina.

BETTINA
Marie's thrilled. I don't know what's wrong with you –

7.5.

RUDOLPH
And you –
Do you live alone in – ?
Don't you have anyone to –

7.6.

Corinna shakes her head.

7.7.

CORINNA
I've been on my own for many years.

RUDOLPH
Like me –

7.8.

That could be the moment for Rudolph to take her hand –
but it's too early for that.

7.9.

Albert and Bettina in the kitchen.

ALBERT
Like a seventeen-year-old tart. And he's behaving like a –

7.10.

RUDOLPH
A long, lonely time.
For I don't know how many years –

CORINNA
A man like you with so much –

7.11.

She looks at him.

7.12.

RUDOLPH
A hard time, as hard as iron.

CORINNA
Yes. A time as hard as iron.

7.13.

BETTINA
Be glad. At least we've got some peace.

7.14.

CORINNA
I can come here occasionally but I get the feeling I'm not
wanted. I am tolerated but I'm also humiliated –

7.15.

Her tone is bitter for a brief moment.

7.16.

CORINNA
Yes – humiliated.

7.17.

In the kitchen.

BETTINA
She's excited –
A man's making advances to her, a man in the prime of life, a
doctor – and my mother always wanted a doctor, look at him,
elegant, educated, charming –

ALBERT
Charming? He's not charming at all. He just pretends to be
and he's not in the prime of life, he's over a HUNDRED.

BETTINA
I think he looks fifty –

7.18.

Albert feels a new spasm of tension in his chest and stomach.

7.19.

In the living room.

RUDOLPH
Families break apart. And that makes people desperate
in their loneliness. Desperate and unprotected. Especially
women. But men are exactly the same too.

7.20.

He drinks some wine.

7.21.

RUDOLPH
There are so many of them out there.
So many lost people, lonely people. A whole army of the
lonely, the defenceless, the weak, the betrayed, who just need
to join forces. Don't you think?

7.22.

BETTINA
Albert – can I ask you something –

ALBERT
What?

7.23.

RUDOLPH
A few hours ago I was one of them myself, in a train stuck in
between stations.
And then I meet you.

7.24.

He takes her hand.

7.25.

RUDOLPH
Gudrun.
The day before Christmas and there's not a single train
running. Everything is falling apart. All those people not
knowing where to go. Incredible. Thank you. Thank you for
everything. Where would I be now without you –

CORINNA
Don't you have anyone, anyone who – Have you no children
–

RUDOLPH
Me – no. No children.

CORINNA plucks up her courage.
No wife waiting for you in – Paraguay.

RUDOLPH
Oh, no, no, no. No wife in Paraguay.

7.26.

BETTINA
Can I ask you something?

ALBERT
What?

BETTINA
When – when have you ever seen my mother's eyes light up
like this?
Ever?

7.27.

RUDOLPH
Right now I'd probably be eating alone in some restaurant.

CORINNA
That is the worst.

RUDOLPH
But that a woman like you –

CORINNA
I've heard that one before.

7.28.

> Rudolph shakes his head slowly although he doesn't know
> exactly what she means.

7.29.

CORINNA
Bettina's father left when she was still a child –

RUDOLPH
You've been through a lot.

CORINNA
A bit.
But not that much. No reason to complain.

7.30.

> Corinna smiles bitterly and shakes her head at the same time.
> She smiles a pained smile which she has seen in the cinema.
> American films.
> The child shouts from her bedroom: Grandmaaa! Grandmaaa!

7.31.

CORINNA
You see – no reason to complain.

7.32.

> She stands up.

7.33.

CORINNA
I'll be right back.

8.1.

> Albert in the bathroom again. Another wave of spasms.
> Shortness of breath, sweating, stomach pains.
> He holds the new tablets up next to the old ones. The old ones
> are white. The new ones are blue.
> The doctor had said: one of the blue ones every day.
> Preferably in the evening. You can take two, but no more –
> sometimes they might make you a bit light-headed – it can
> happen.
> Albert tries to phone his doctor. He puts his reading glasses
> on. He takes his reading glasses off.
> The mobile phone. The surgery answerphone.

"The surgery is now closed."
Albert sits down on the edge of the bath. He takes one of the
blue pills. He takes one of the white pills.
It is 8.05 p.m.

8.2.

At the same time in the living room. Rudolph alone.
He stands in front of the large oil painting, looking at it. He
looks at it for a long time.
Bettina enters the living room with a large cardboard box
which she carries into the kitchen. 'Christmas tree decorations'
is written on the box in large letters. She remembers that
Albert and she have to decorate the tree today, that the tree
is still in the car and then she remembers her conversation
with the producer again. With the box in her hands she thinks
about the phrase: "the end of the world".

RUDOLPH
What a picture!

BETTINA
Yes, it was painted by a friend of ours –

8.3.

Bettina disappears into the kitchen. Her back in silhouette.

8.4.

RUDOLPH
Painted –

8.5.

Bettina comes out of the kitchen. Relaxed for a moment.

8.6.

BETTINA
It's one of his best works –

8.7.

Albert in the bathroom. He takes another of the blue and
another of the white pills.
He feels better, although he can't be feeling better because of
the pills yet.
His mobile phone is next to the wash basin. He checks to see
if he has got a text.

No, he hasn't had any texts.

8.8.

At the same time in the living room.

RUDOLPH
And what's the name of this artist?

BETTINA
Konrad.

8.9.

Bettina's husband is in the bathroom. She's wondering where he's got to. Her mother is in her daughter's room. Their guest is alone.

8.10

RUDOLPH
Konrad...

BETTINA
Are you interested in art?

RUDOLPH
Essentially I'm more interested in artists.
In the person behind the picture. I tend to see the person more than the picture –

8.11.

He laughs.

8.12.

RUDOLPH
I am a doctor after all.

BETTINA
You'll get to meet him in a minute – He's going to be coming round. The man has a terrible inferiority complex –

RUDOLPH
Yes, clearly –
As so often. Unfortunately.

BETTINA laughs.
I think sometimes he thinks he's a nobody and he suffers because of it –

8.13.

She wonders why she's telling him this.

8.14.

RUDOLPH
Like so many –
How could it be otherwise – the picture reveals that –

8.15.

He points at the picture.

8.16.

RUDOLPH
I had suspected that. Some of them tend to think too much of
themselves, others make themselves suffer, and not everyone
has the vocation they believe that they have. What's the
painting called?

BETTINA
The struggle.

RUDOLPH
My Struggle?

BETTINA
No!

8.17.

She laughs out loud.

8.18.

BETTINA
THE struggle, not MY struggle.

RUDOLPH
The struggle –
Often the psyche follows reality – we think of the psyche as a
highly complex entity – yes, of course –
dreams, desires, instincts, neuroses, fears –

8.19.

He leaves the sentence hanging in the air.

8.20.

RUDOLPH

But the truth is the psyche is no more than a mirror of reality.
The man feels inferior?
Perhaps he's right.
Perhaps because he knows he's not happy.
Perhaps because he knows he's not doing what he ought to do
in his life.

8.21.

Albert appears in the doorway with a red wine glass and a full
bottle of red wine. It is 8.08 p.m.
Rudolph continues.

8.22.

RUDOLPH

Perhaps because he knows he will never be happy. Perhaps
because he knows he is not a great artist.
Look, this artificiality, this distortion of everything beautiful –
He suffers because of this –
And he won't allow himself to take the decisive step –

8.23.

Rudolph turns to Albert.

8.24.

RUDOLPH

Not the picture, no, *he*, the artist is lacking something – he is
not what he wants to be, not what he could be – only very few
people understand the true nature of their task!

ALBERT

Their task, what task – what does this task consist of then?

RUDOLPH

The task! What does the task consist of?! Let me ask you!
What does your task consist of, Albert?
You know, you have understood. I can tell from one look at
this bookshelf, at your books: Gudrun has told me who you –
What an impressive series of – well – it is our task to carry
light into the darkness. Is it not?

8.25.

Before Albert can answer:

8.26.

BETTINA
We've got to put up the tree.

RUDOLPH
The tree! Oh God, the tree! I'm talking and talking and
stopping you from –
If there's any way I can make myself useful –

8.27.

He looks towards the door.
Corinna and the child come back into the living room in a
good mood –

8.28.

CORINNA proud
We've got everything planned –

BETTINA
What?

8.29.

The child says: we're going ice skating.

8.30.

BETTINA
When? Now?

CORINNA
Now? Not now. On her birthday of course.

ALBERT
But, but – after what happened last year –

CORINNA
What happened?

BETTINA
Let's get Christmas over with first.

CORINNA
We – we want to go ice skating just like last year – you don't

need to come too! And afterwards I'll take Marie and her
friends –

8.31.

The child is thrilled.

8.32.

BETTINA
We wanted to do something different this time –
Didn't you say that this year you –

8.33.

But ice skating is nice, the child says.

8.34.

CORINNA winking at Rudolph.
I hope you know how to skate –

8.35.

8.12 p.m.
Albert feels slightly giddy.

8.36.

CORINNA
Where's the Christmas tree?
Haven't you got a Christmas tree?

9.1.

Bach: Well-Tempered Clavier Book 1 Prelude and Fugue No.
1 in C major.
A couple of minutes later. Two men in the street outside the
building. In the darkness of the night one of the men wipes
the snow off the bonnet of a large estate car. It's a big old
Volvo. The other man stands beside the car. He's not wearing
the right shoes.
The car's lock is frozen. The man who wiped the snow off the
car, Albert, looks up at the large windows of the apartment.
The child is standing upstairs by the window and waves to
them.

9.2.

At the same time in the kitchen. Bettina and Corinna.
Corinna with a glass of red wine in her hand and a cigarette.

Bettina is also drinking and picks the box with the Christmas tree decorations up off the floor and puts it on the table. She considers unpacking the Christmas tree decorations but doesn't do it.

9.3.

CORINNA
They want to get rid of me.
It's perfectly obvious.
And I can't get by on the money anyway.
Mhm.

9.4.

CORINNA blows smoke in the air in irritation.

9.5.

The man in the street next to the frozen car shouts something up towards the window, but the child can't understand what he is saying. Wait, the other man says, the man who doesn't have the right shoes, I've got an idea. He picks a hip flask out of his jacket pocket. Alcohol! He laughs. To Gudrun! What a glorious woman. You should be happy! Not everyone has a mother-in-law like that!

9.6.

In the kitchen.

CORINNA
And that's the worst thing. Those people are the worst, honestly.
All of them.
Meinrat says I'm the best.

BETTINA
It doesn't sound like he wants to get rid of you.

CORINNA
He says I'm impossible to ignore.

9.7.

She laughs coarsely.

9.8.

CORINNA
He keeps looking at my cleavage.

BETTINA amused.
Really. Well there is plenty of it. After all.

CORINNA
He says he can't resist.
He thinks it's funny.

BETTINA
If you don't like the job, we can look for something else for
you.
Albert knows enough people. Or you can just stop –

CORINNA
I've brought a child up on my own and my pension still isn't
enough – otherwise I wouldn't have to go in there.

BETTINA
If you need more money you only have to say.

CORINNA
And then sit around at home all day?

9.9.

Albert and Rudolph have got the boot open. Rudolph waves
to the child at the window. They drag the very large Christmas
tree out of the car.

9.10.

RUDOLPH
How lovely to have a family.

9.11.

They've got the tree out of the car. The tree is now standing
next to the car. It is still snowing. Rudolph is freezing, but he's
in a good mood.

9.12.

RUDOLPH
Wonderful. I wish you could have met my father.

ALBERT
Your father –

RUDOLPH
My father was an – an expert in these areas. As you can
imagine –

9.13.

Rudolph offers Albert a swig from his hipflask. Albert shakes
his head.

9.14.

ALBERT
In which areas –

RUDOLPH
In your area –
'History of Human Experiments', 'Dictatorship and Death'.
'Human Dignity'. 'The Future of the Past'.
But the past is the past. No doubt about that. Is there?

9.15.

Albert does not answer.

9.16.

RUDOLPH
Is there?

ALBERT
No, no.

RUDOLPH
No?

ALBERT
The past does not exist.

RUDOLPH
Oh really?

ALBERT
No – it haunts us and that makes it part of the present.

9.17.

The two men lift the tree onto their shoulders. Albert is
allergic to pine trees, especially when he touches them. He can
immediately feel welts forming on his neck and his hands.

9.18.

> RUDOLPH
> An interesting view. You think the past is never over.
>
> ALBERT
> Worse than that.

9.19.

> In the kitchen.
>
> CORINNA
> They'll evict me from the flat.
>
> BETTINA
> You've been saying that for thirty years.

9.20.

> In the street. The men with the Christmas tree. Albert's hands and neck are itching.

9.21.

> RUDOLPH laughs.
> Ha! You're perfectly right!

9.22.

> BETTINA
> You've been saying that for thirty years.
> And it's not true.
>
> CORINNA
> It is true –
>
> BETTINA
> They can't throw you out.
>
> CORINNA
> But, but –

9.23.

> Corinna takes a quick drink and a drag on her cigarette.

9.24.

> In the street.
>
> RUDOLPH
> Part of us! Yes, of course – but –

9.25.

In the kitchen.

CORINNA
I can't afford the flat any more. And they put the rent up
every year.
They know very well I can't manage any more.

BETTINA
If you wouldn't keep lying the whole time.

CORINNA
When, when have I lied.

9.26.

Corinna laughs bitterly. She has another drink.

9.27.

The men in the snow with the Christmas tree make their way
to the front door. The itching. Albert tries to carry the tree and
scratch his neck at the same time. He slips. The tree almost
falls on top of him.

9.28.

RUDOLPH
Careful!

9.29.

In the kitchen. Corinna perking up briefly.

CORINNA
Alright, alright.

9.30.

She has another drink.

9.31.

In the snow. The men make their way to the front door.

9.32.

RUDOLPH
Can you manage?

9.33.

Albert scratches his neck.

9.34.

RUDOLPH
Is that an allergy?

9.35.

In the kitchen.

CORINNA
Haven't you got an ashtray?

BETTINA
Yes, mother. We have got an ashtray, it's right next to you.

9.36.

The men with the tree in the stairwell. The light goes off. No switch near them.

9.37.

RUDOLPH
Is everything alright?

9.38.

They climb the stairs with the tree in the dark.

9.39.

RUDOLPH
I mean, is one allowed to kill a human being? No! But sometimes it has to be done – Sometimes perhaps it has to be done. If it serves a higher cause.

ALBERT
What cause.

RUDOLPH
Jesus. For example. Was killed. By his own father.

9.40.

In the kitchen.

BETTINA
How long are you staying?

CORINNA
I can leave.

BETTINA
That's not what I said.

9.41.

A bitter moment in which angry memories surface on both sides. Both try to pull themselves together. Tomorrow's Christmas.
At that moment Bettina's mobile phone makes a noise. She has received a text. Bettina reads the text and smiles.

9.42.

CORINNA
Who's that from?

9.43.

The look on her daughter's face.

9.44.

Albert comes rushing into the kitchen and washes his neck, face and hands.

CORINNA
Phew –

9.45.

Then Albert goes to the fridge and takes another pill.

9.46.

ALBERT
It itches.

CORINNA
Why?

ALBERT
The tree –

CORINNA
Ah –

9.47.

Albert washes his neck again.

9.48.

CORINNA
Is there anything you're not allergic to?

BETTINA
Red wine –

CORINNA
Aren't you going to eat anything today?

BETTINA
Yes – we just weren't expecting visitors.

CORINNA
How nice of you to leave me standing outside the door for so long.

BETTINA
I was on the phone.

CORINNA
Yes, yes. You're always on the phone when I come.

10.1.

8.40 p.m. In the living room:
Rudolph is playing the piano. Prelude and Fugue no. 16 in G minor, BWV 861.
His hands glide across the keyboard.
Corinna stands next to the piano watching him.

10.2.

In the bathroom. Running water.
Albert examines his hands and neck. There's not much to see.
He leans on the washbasin. He turns the tap off.
Then he phones someone. His face in the mirror.
He says, hey.
And the woman on the other end says, hey Albi.
He takes a short, deep breath.
He says: don't call me Albi, please,
and she says, why not, what don't you like about it.

10.3.

His father had called him Albi. His father who killed himself when Albert was six years old.

10.4.

He says, I don't like anything about it, how are you,
and she says: fine, fine, I'm at my parents' house. We're just
about to eat. My mother's had too much to drink and now she
wants us all to pray and it's not even Christmas till tomorrow.
I've got to put up the Christmas tree in a minute, he says, and
I'm allergic to the thing.
He laughs.
She says: put rubber gloves on. You're not allergic to rubber.
Are you?
She laughs. He laughs too, quietly.

10.5.

Some time later. Albert and Rudolph, putting the Christmas
tree up in the living room. Albert is wearing yellow rubber
gloves.
Bettina and Corinna and the child watch.
Corinna's face looking at the gloves.

10.6.

BETTINA
And you really are from Paraguay.

10.7

Bettina is suddenly in a better mood. Why?

10.8.

Much later that night. Albert and Bettina alone.

ALBERT
You know what kind of people live in Paraguay?

BETTINA
No idea, Paraguayans?!

ALBERT
Yes, but he's NOT a Paraguayan.

10.9.

In the living room putting up the tree.

RUDOLPH
I was born there. But as you can see I'm not a Paraguayan. My
ancestors emigrated.

ALBERT
Your ancestors –

RUDOLPH
Yes –

10.10.

Rudolph knows what the other man is thinking.

10.11.

BETTINA
In Paraguay, how unusual –

RUDOLPH laughs.
But we always had a Christmas tree.

10.12.

A little earlier. The voice on the phone after a brief pause:
Thanks for the money, she says, but I don't want any money
from you.
– It's your Christmas money –
– Not very romantic, don't you think?
– No, no, don't say that, you've –
In the bathroom. The woman Albert is talking to on the
phone has been working for him at the publisher's for four
months. Naomi. And it quickly became clear that he and
Naomi –
Albert's face in the mirror.

10.13.

In the living room. Some time later. Albert with the rubber
gloves. The two men putting up the tree. Albert tries not to
touch the tree. He particularly tries to avoid the branches
touching his face, which is almost impossible.
Corinna observes the situation, drinks some red wine.
Bettina gives instructions, which side of the tree should face
the front and is also drinking red wine.

BETTINA
Left, left – no to the le-eft, not the right –

10.14.

The voice on the phone:
– How's your wife?
– I don't know, let's not talk about my wife.

– No, why not, Albi?
Silence.
– I'm going to be going out later, she says.
– Where?
– With a couple of friends.
– Aha.
– Yes, we'll have a few drinks and see –
– Okay. Well, take care.
– What do you mean by that?
– Just –
– Are you afraid I might do something –
– Yeah – Where are you going, I could drop by.
– You? I think we're better off keeping that separate.
– Do I embarrass you? Too old?
– You're old but that doesn't bother me. Really.
He says nothing. She says: What about you? Does your wife
give you a Christmas fuck? I keep imagining you doing it with
her. Is she any good?

10.15.

The men turn the tree. Bettina provides instructions. Left,
you're turning it to the right, left!
Albert disagrees.
Corinna disagrees with Albert. Albert says something and
scratches his face. Bettina disagrees. Corinna laughs at Albert's
suggestion and shakes her head. She says he doesn't know the
difference between left and right!

10.16.

RUDOLPH
Well, yes, well, Paraguay – it's just a country like any other,
though I must admit I didn't choose it – my father –

10.17.

The tree slowly falls over. Slow motion.

10.18.

RUDOLPH
Ooops!

10.19.

Everyone laughs apart from Albert who is stressed.

10.20.

A few minutes earlier. In the bathroom. Albert's face in the mirror. He is on the phone.
– And what about your wife? Does your wife give you a Christmas fuck? I keep imagining you doing it with her. Is she any good?
He says: Oh God, don't say things like that.
– I miss you.
– I miss you too, Albi, says the voice at the other end.
She's crying, he thinks and she says: How's your daughter, Albi, sorry, I'm not supposed to say Albi, what does your daughter call you, does she call you Daddy, I'd like a Daddy like you.

10.21.

Marie, Albert's daughter, in the kitchen.
The girl's hands putting a plate on the table.
The glasses. Albert takes off his rubber gloves.
Rudolph and Albert and Corinna and Bettina and Marie lay the table in the kitchen for supper.

10.22.

A couple of minute earlier. In the bathroom. Albert says:
I think your Dad's a bit older than me.
– Maybe. Not much.

10.23.

The fridge opens and closes. Hands. The child's hands, the father's hands, the mother's, the grandmother's hands with the large rings Bettina hates so much. Plates. The table is laid. Glasses. Wine. Water. Cheese. Cold meat. Fish. Bread. Butter.

10.24.

CORINNA
How beautiful it sounds. Paraguay.
I never got away from here –

BETTINA
Where did you want to go? Paraguay?
Home was like Paraguay for us –

CORINNA
What do you mean by that?

10.25.

The grandmother, nervously looking for cutlery in the drawer.

10.26.

CORINNA
Haven't you got any knives?

10.27.

The child, fetching the knives from the drawer.

10.28.

In the bathroom.
The woman on the phone says:
You're a good man, Albert. But don't give me money.
– I'm sorry.
– That's okay. Thank you.

10.29.

In the kitchen. It is 9.10 p.m.
The doorbell.
Bettina looks at the clock.

10.30.

BETTINA
That's Konrad.

ALBERT
I'll get it.

BETTINA
No, no, I'm on my way.

10.31.

Bettina goes to the door, closing the kitchen door behind her.
Albert watches her.

11.1.

Bettina in the entrance hall by the door to the apartment. A
quick look in the round mirror next to the door. She smooths
out her blouse.
She opens the door. In front of her stands Konrad, the painter
who painted the large picture which is hanging in the living
room.

Konrad and Albert have been friends since they were children.

– Hey. She says this "Hey" smiling and serious.

Bettina visited Konrad in his studio a couple of days ago. It was an afternoon of very few words. He told her that he was in love with her, he had been for a very long time, and she said nothing. She just looked at him.

Hey, he answers, her husband's friend for so many years. The light in the doorway goes out. He stands in front of her on the stairs in the dark. A yellow strip of light spills out of the apartment onto the red carpet running up the steps of the old stairway.

– You're standing in the dark.

He shrugs his shoulders.

– That stair light's never worked.

Konrad is unshaven, he is wearing the overalls he usually wears for painting. She can see traces of oil paint on his hands. She smiles. She says:

You look really Christmassy.

He says: I know. He's hiding something behind his back and now he reveals the present: it is a paintbrush. He holds it like a bunch of flowers.

She laughs out loud.

– Hey!

– Yup, he says.

– What's that?

– It's a present. For you.

– Thank you.

– It's a paintbrush.

– I can see that!

She is perplexed. Now something happens that she hadn't planned. She pushes him into the darkness of the doorway and kisses him. It is the first time they have kissed. He is just as surprised as she is. After a moment they pull away from each other.

She says:

– Thank you. What a beautiful present.

11.2.

Everyone around the table in the kitchen/dining room:
Laughter. Albert, Bettina,
Corinna, Rudolph, the child, Konrad.

It is 9.17 p.m. Albert puts on his reading glasses and reads the label on the bottle of red wine in front of him, though he knows what it says, after all he bought the wine.

RUDOLPH
And I said if no one comes to rescue us, we'll have to continue the journey on foot!

CORINNA laughs, almost snorting.
On foot! In the snow!

RUDOLPH
Still. It was very beautiful. The two of us alone in the train compartment and outside the blue light of dusk, the snow – I love the North. Gudrun –

ALBERT
Corinna. She's called Corinna.

RUDOLPH
But Gudrun – it's such a beautiful name, almost a sacred name, don't you know that
–

11.3.

Rudolph looks at Konrad. Konrad shrugs his shoulders. He tries to make eye contact with Bettina.

11.4.

KONRAD
Gudrun?

RUDOLPH
Gudrun means – "battle" and "magic", so it means "the magician of battle" in Old High German, or in Swedish it means: "She, who knows the secret of the Gods." Isn't that beautiful? These old names – they are the legacy of our ancestors and we must preserve that legacy –
And she looked – Gudrun – she had wrapped herself up in my coat, it was getting dark and icy patterns were forming on the windows of the train compartment, she looked – she looked like a queen –

11.5.

Corinna is happy. She is beaming. Rudolph smiles.

11.6.

RUDOLPH
And at the moment you're really writing about – Gudrun told
me that you're currently writing about –

CORINNA laughing and mocking.
'Christmas in Auschwitz' – that's what his new book is
supposed to be called, well, well, what a subject – how can
you spend all day –

11.7.

She laughs again. Rudolph laughs too.

11.8.

ALBERT
I –

11.9.

Bettina has heard this before. Her mother never talks about
the films Bettina makes. But she likes talking about Albert's
work, in terms which are both admiring and derogatory at the
same time.

11.10.

ALBERT
Well – at the moment, I –

11.11.

He's laughing but at the same time he is annoyed. He never
talks about his work to strangers.

11.12.

RUDOLPH
Tell me, I'm very interested in these historical subjects –

11.13.

Albert tells a story which Bettina has heard many times.
Albert always tells this story when someone asks him what
he's currently working on. In different variations. He tells the
story well, with pauses for effect. He likes it.

11.14.

ALBERT
Well, I – I, what I'm writing about – I was having lunch one day recently, on my own, at the Italian place on the corner by the publisher's and I was making notes, working on a manuscript – corrections, comments, footnotes, the way you do – and in the end this page of manuscript looked like – like some schizophrenic –

11.15.

Konrad laughs.

11.16.

ALBERT
– the page looked like the sketch of some global conspiracy, covered in arrows and circles and crosses –

11.17.

For a second Albert suddenly feels that slight dizziness again, a faint instability in his body – as if he were falling into an endless void.
Konrad carries on laughing.

11.18.

KONRAD
Arrows and circles and crosses – like some –

11.19.

Konrad and Bettina's eyes meet.

11.20.

ALBERT
Well, everyone has their themes – And the waiter eventually caught sight of the page and said: "Ma dottore," –

11.21.

Albert makes a typically Italian hand movement.

11.22.

ALBERT
And then he stuck his finger on a place on the page and said: "I thinka here is missing a little amore."

11.23.

Albert laughs. The others except Bettina and the child laugh.

11.24.1.

ALBERT
– yes – the page looked like some global conspiracy and that
was just the table of contents –

11.24.2.

Rudolph smiles at the story.

11.24.3.

RUDOLPH
And you?

11.25.

Bettina's foot momentarily touches Konrad's leg under the
table.

11.26.

KONRAD
Me?

RUDOLPH
What do you do?

KONRAD
I paint –

RUDOLPH
You paint – yes, of course, you're the – you're the painter –

KONRAD
Yes –

RUDOLPH
We've talked about you – Bettina and I –

KONRAD
Oh yes?

RUDOLPH
Of course! Your picture's impossible to ignore!

11.27.

Rudolph laughs. Konrad is uncertain. Bettina smiles at him. Albert notices her look. Something irritates him but he doesn't know what. He briefly feels a little dizzy again.

11.28.

Some time later. In the living room. Bettina and Albert alone for a moment.

BETTINA
Look.

ALBERT
Hm?

BETTINA
Konrad gave us a present.

11.29.

She shows him the paintbrush.

11.30.

ALBERT
Aha –

BETTINA
Were you talking to someone on the phone before when you were in the bathroom?

ALBERT
Yes – the publishers. Why?

BETTINA
Nice, isn't it?

ALBERT
It's a paintbrush.

BETTINA
Exactly.

11.31.

In the kitchen.

RUDOLPH
And what do you paint?

KONRAD
Frictions.

RUDOLPH
Frictions?

11.32.

Corinna's made-up mouth. She laughs in a silly, knowing way.
Konrad is disconcerted.

11.33.

KONRAD
Frictions. Oppositions, tensions, everything and nothing –
wanting and not being able to, not being allowed –

11.34.

He drinks tragically. The glass in his hand. The glass at his
mouth.

11.35.

KONRAD
How can I describe it –
What do you do for a living?

CORINNA
He's a doctor –

RUDOLPH
You paint abstracts –

KONRAD
No –

RUDOLPH
But that painting in the living room is an abstract –

KONRAD
No, it would be abstract if it abstracted something –

RUDOLPH
Excuse me for interrupting you, Konrad, may I call you
Konrad? May I ask you something?

KONRAD
Of course –

RUDOLPH
What do you want?

11.36.

> Albert laughs. Bettina touches Konrad's hand briefly as if by accident.

11.37.

KONRAD
What do I want?

RUDOLPH
I think that's something every artist asks himself – What do you want from art?

KONRAD
I – I want to paint –

RUDOLPH
Yes, of course, that's your talent, but what else do you want?!

KONRAD
Well, – the things that I want aren't things you can go looking for – you can only –

11.38.

> Some time later. Albert and Bettina alone for a moment in the living room. Bettina with the paintbrush in her hand.

ALBERT
He's drunk my red wine for twenty-five years and now he gives us a paintbrush.

BETTINA
He did give us a picture as well.

ALBERT
Thank God this time it's only a paintbrush. If it was a picture we'd have to hang it up.

11.39.

> She hugs him.

11.40.

BETTINA
Bad mood?

ALBERT
Me?

BETTINA
You're in a bad mood.

ALBERT
No. But your mother –

BETTINA
Jealous?

ALBERT
Of your mother?

BETTINA
Of the paintbrush?

11.41.

Albert looks at her. Why did she say that?

11.42.

ALBERT
No!

BETTINA
Yes you are –

ALBERT
A paintbrush is a paintbrush.
It's what you do with it that counts.

12.1.

Flashback. A few days earlier.
Konrad and Albert in Albert's study. More bookshelves. A
large desk. Outside it is dark. The desk lamp is the only light.
Albert and Konrad are drinking cognac. Albert is looking for
something.

12.2.

KONRAD
A paintbrush is a paintbrush.
It's what you do with it that counts.
Being able to produce, you know, production, working, the
work is sacred.

12.3.

Albert has found what he was looking for: a bundle of
banknotes, which he gives to Konrad. It's not the first time
he's lent Konrad money. No – it's more the rule. Konrad takes
the money.

12.4.

KONRAD
Just till the beginning of the month – thanks – The work is
sacred, – it's the only thing that's sacred to me –

12.5.

Slightly hoarse.

12.6.

KONRAD
More sacred than friendship, more sacred than alcohol.

12.7.

Konrad drinks.

12.8.

KONRAD
The depths of the personal, of pain. Loss. The horror of being
alone in front of a canvas –

ALBERT
The horror of being alone.

12.9.

Albert smiles and drinks cognac.

12.10.

KONRAD
This loneliness which seems to swallow you up. Desire. The
night. What's unsaid. What can't be said. The secrets.

12.11.

Konrad holds his cognac glass up to the light from the desk
lamp. The large windows. The snow outside.
Albert has heard all this before.

12.12.

ALBERT
The secrets.

12.13.

Konrad pours himself more cognac. Albert thinks Konrad is
drinking too fast, that he'd probably already been drinking
before he arrived. Once he's reached a certain level of
drunkenness, Konrad has been saying the same thing for
years. He talks mainly about himself. Konrad always wanted
to paint and Albert always wanted to write. Both of them have
managed to achieve what they always wanted to do with their
lives but Konrad still isn't happy with what he is doing. And
he doesn't earn any money.

12.14.

KONRAD
Secrets are freedom. Aren't they?

12.15.

He looks Albert in the eye.

12.16.

KONRAD
But what can a picture do?
A paintbrush is just a paintbrush.
A picture can't do anything.

12.17.

Bitter.

12.18.

KONRAD
Nothing.
I should pack it in. But there's nothing else I can do.

12.19.

Konrad drinks again.

12.20.

KONRAD
Nothing's worse than self-pity. If I could write. If I could find
words for the truth. You're looking for the truth. You always were.

And you haven't got a clue what the truth is. But still. You're looking for it. That's the difference.

12.21.

The night before Christmas.
Bettina in the bathroom, she looks at herself briefly in the bathroom mirror. She is pleased with the paintbrush.

12.21.2.

A film in black and white.
Rain on the large windows of a studio.
Pictures, paints, papers, canvases, sketches, paintbrushes, mess.
Scattered across the floor:
hastily removed clothes,
a woman's elegant suit, stockings,
a set of overalls.

12.22.

In the study. The light of the desk lamp.

KONRAD
And you haven't got a clue what the truth is. But still. You're looking for it. That's the difference.
I was born in the wrong time.
Art is nothing. Art is dead. It's killed itself off.

12.23.

The night before Christmas. Rudolph and Corinna in the kitchen.
Corinna's eyes are gleaming.
She laughs animatedly.

CORINNA
This man – this man –

12.24.

She means Konrad.

12.25.

CORINNA
This man talks nothing but rubbish. Always has done.

13.1.

In the kitchen. Everyone is having supper.

Rudolph describes the beginning of an opera which he would
have liked to have composed, if only he could compose.
Corinna and the child listen in raptures – as do the others.

RUDOLPH
Very quietly,
very, very quietly:

13.2.

Very quietly. He's almost whispering.

13.3.

RUDOLPH
Music.
The violins. A high note, a fluttering.
You know how violins sound –

13.4.

He plays an invisible violin and sings to imitate the sound of a
violin. Everyone is amazed.

13.5.

RUDOLPH
Then the cellos:

13.6.

He sings a slowly rising cello phrase, three or four notes, no
more.

13.7.

RUDOLPH
A measured tempo,
not too loud,
not too loud,
the cello theme is repeated,
a rising series of notes,
almost like a slow march.
One can sense:
it's before dawn.

13.8.

Rudolph takes a breath. He pauses for a moment, full of
reverence, and looks around the group.

13.9.

RUDOLPH
Before dawn.
Now:
the double basses,
reminding us of the dark night
the night –
crescendo
the double basses
reminding us of bad dreams,
of everything
one would rather forget,
the cigarettes and the wine,
and then the bad dreams,
but now,
the cellos again, the violas and the violins,
now the night is over,
sunrise.

13.10.

He repeats the phrases of the string instruments.

13.11.

RUDOLPH
Now the night is over.
The brass enters,
first the horns, still restrained,
then the trumpets,

13.12.

Becoming louder.

13.13.

RUDOLPH
Sun, light,
trumpets,
trumpets,
sun, light,
a high mountain wind,
at sunrise,
a cloudless day,
icy,
clear,

and on the peaks:
snow.

13.14.

Bettina and Albert a moment later alone in the entrance hall.
She giggles happily:

BETTINA
He's mad.

ALBERT:
He's not mad, he's dangerous –

BETTINA suddenly humourless.
You think everyone's dangerous.

13.15.

In the kitchen. A little earlier. Rudolph continues.

RUDOLPH
What a day,
so cold and clear and bright,
a few bars of solo violin,
and one can hear the sound of the mountain stream –

13.16.

He imitates the sound of the mountain stream.

13.17.

RUDOLPH
And one can see, or one would be able to see –
front left,
almost leaning against the sheer rock face,
a modest inn.
Or a hut, a modest farmhouse –
The morning sun on the mountains,
which were already there
before the first human being walked the earth,
and which still will be there,
once the last human being has passed.
A wanderer
on the narrow mountain path
on the edge of the abyss,
a lonely wanderer in the early hours,

who knows,

perhaps he was travelling all night,
in the darkness.
Where has he come from?
What is he carrying?
A bundle? A box?

But the mountains are feared
for sudden changes in the weather,
at present the sky
is still cloudless
and suddenly a storm comes –
Now there would be drums,
drums,

13.18.

Rudolph drums on the table. To the child.

13.19.

RUDOLPH
You can drum too!
And you, Corinna, the violins –

13.20.

Rudolph sings the voice of the violins.
Corinna sings the voice of the violins back, rather hoarsely.

13.21.

RUDOLPH
Bettina! The violins!
Konrad,
the double basses,
the cellos,
the violins at a high tempo,
at the tempo
of the wall of cloud racing onwards,
what had just been a bright sky
darkens,
a storm approaches,
icy cold,
snow and ice.

13.22.

Bettina and Albert alone.

ALBERT
Something's not right about him.

13.23.

In the kitchen.

RUDOLPH
The threat of death,
trombones,
horns,
and with the last of his strength
the lonely wanderer reaches
the shelter,
the wanderer has to
reach the shelter –
one can see it,
don't forget,
front left,
almost leaning on the sheer rock face,
the modest hut,
the sanctuary of an inn.
The wanderer collapses
outside the doorway which is his salvation
and then a woman
comes rushing out of the door,
one can see her blonde hair,
her dress in the wind –

ALBERT
I thought it was cold –

RUDOLPH continues without being distracted.
– here the melody of a folk song wafts in out of nothing,
possibly a flute –

13.24.

The child asks: And then? And then?

13.25.

RUDOLPH
And the brass again,
the violins in the storm,
the basses,
Konrad!

13.26.

Konrad sings.

13.27.

RUDOLPH
Corinna!

13.28.

Corinna quickly drinks some wine and sings.

13.29.

CORINNA
How beautiful.

13.30.

The little girl is thrilled.
RUDOLPH breaks off in the middle and shouts joyously:
Children!

13.31.

RUDOLPH
Children!
Let us celebrate –

13.32.

The child is surprised by the man shouting "children!" but she
also thinks it's funny. It is an unusual expression in her family.
Sometimes her father says: "comrades", and sometimes he
says: "brothers and sisters" and she now understands that this
is a joke because she doesn't have any brothers or sisters.

13.33.

RUDOLPH
Let's celebrate!

CORINNA
Yes, let's, what are we celebrating –

ALBERT
Strictly speaking Christmas isn't until tomorrow –

KONRAD
Well for me –

RUDOLPH
Never mind!
Let's celebrate the solstice.

CORINNA
Oooh! The solstice –

ALBERT
According to the calendar –

RUDOLPH
The calendar!

ALBERT
According to the calendar the solstice was –

CORINNA
Oh –

RUDOLPH
One has to celebrate festivals as they fall and when a new, better time is dawning the exact day doesn't matter, let's not tyrannize ourselves with punctuality, the solstice –

13.34.

The child asks: So when is the solstice –
And Albert thinks, I explained that to her a couple of days ago – she knows that –

13.35.

RUDOLPH
The solstice is an ancient, sacred festival –

13.36.

Some time later. Bettina and Albert alone for a moment by the bookshelves.

ALBERT
These Nordic gods, the solstice, it's all –

13.37.

RUDOLPH
In the summer the night of the solstice marks the longest day and afterwards the days get shorter again but in winter, now, in December, the solstice means that the days will get longer again, longer and longer until those glorious northern nights when it never gets truly dark.

13.38.

Rudolph takes a drink. The red wine is delicious. A wine from the Languedoc.

13.39.

RUDOLPH
To summer.
To light.
To the long Northern days.
To Odin.

KONRAD
I tried to paint midsummer night once.

CORINNA
The white nights.

ALBERT
And?

KONRAD
How can you capture it – that primordial light.

13.40.

Rudolph makes an odd face. Primordial light reminds him of Gustav Mahler and Rudolph hates Gustav Mahler.

13.41.

ALBERT
Primordial light.

13.42.

Bettina starts taking the Christmas tree decorations out of the box and putting them on the table.

13.43.

CORINNA
What are you doing?

BETTINA
I'm picking out the decorations for the Christmas tree –

CORINNA
Now?

BETTINA
Yes, now, why not?
Am I disturbing anyone –

CORINNA
How inhospitable, we have a visitor – and we're celebrating
the solstice –

13.44.

Her eyes fall on the expensive Christmas tree decorations, on
the old candle holders and the real wax candles which Bettina
is taking out of the box. All wrapped in beautiful, expensive,
soft paper.

13.45.

CORINNA
Well – well –

BETTINA
What?

CORINNA
Well – real candles. Nobody does that any more. Nobody. I
think it's actually banned –

BETTINA
We –

13.46.

Bettina strokes the head of her daughter who is looking with
great big eyes at the antique Christmas tree decorations she
has bought recently. Mother and daughter: a beautiful image.

13.47.

BETTINA
We do it properly.

13.48.1.

Later. Possibly days later. Possibly in a car. It has started to
thaw. Rain. Possibly outside the station. Corinna bitter, alone
with Albert.

13.48.2.

CORINNA
She wasn't always like this. I remember when she was a child.
She didn't confront me then. She didn't stab me in the back in
front of everyone.

13.49.

Albert has heard this many times. He can smell the breath of
the woman who is his wife's mother.

13.50.

CORINNA
What does she do all day?
She buys antique Christmas tree decorations. She buys wax
candles.
It's nothing to do with me but she's throwing money away. *She*
throws money away.

13.51.

In the kitchen.

BETTINA
We – we do it properly.

13.52.

CORINNA needs a moment. Then:

13.53.

CORINNA
What do you mean: "properly".
As if what I'd done in the past was wrong.
I did what I could.
And I didn't have a husband with the bank account to match.
I had to work. I didn't have time.
I couldn't make any boring films nobody wants to watch.

13.54.

Albert and Bettina alone, four minutes later.

BETTINA
It won't be long now before the old girl's sticking her tongue
down his throat.

13.55.

Bettina is in tears.

13.56.

BETTINA
And you don't defend me.

ALBERT
How am I supposed to defend you –

BETTINA
She respects you because you're the one who opens the wine bottles but as soon as you turn your back on her, she'll bite, it happens every time.

13.57.

CORINNA
I did what I could.
And I didn't have a husband with the bank account to match. I had to work. I didn't have time.
I couldn't make any boring films nobody wants to watch.

13.58.

At this moment, within this brief moment, Corinna becomes aware of several things. That she has wounded her daughter deeply. That she loves her daughter. And that she hates her because she hates her life. She would like to take hold of Bettina's hand.
Bettina is missing a new Christmas tree bauble, a valuable, mouth-blown one which she only bought this morning and had put inside the box. This bauble isn't there.

13.59.1.

BETTINA
Did you drop something earlier in the entrance hall?

CORINNA
Me? When? No. Why?

13.59.2.

A woman in her mid-sixties who secretly looks inside a box in an entrance hall, who secretly takes something out of that box which does not belong to her and has nothing to do with her.

She takes something out of the box which then slips out of her hands.

13.59.3.

A glass bauble shattering into a thousand pieces. Slow motion.

13.59.4.

The woman on her knees in the entrance hall nervously and secretly picking up the pieces with her hands. She looks for a bin.

13.60.

In the kitchen. Rudolph turns to the child, who is playing with her toothbrush horse while she is eating.

13.61.

RUDOLPH
And who is that?

13.62.

The child says: This is my horse.

13.63.1.

RUDOLPH
Oh! How lovely. What's your horse called?

13.63.2.

The child says: he's called Cloud.

13.64.

RUDOLPH
I had a horse too. But a real horse.
He was called Loki.

ALBERT
Loki?

RUDOLPH
And what do you want for Christmas?

13.65.

The child says: I'd like a grandfather.

13.66.

CORINNA
Ohooo!

BETTINA
She's been saying that since she was three.
Sometimes she just wants a dog.

13.67.

And then the child starts crying because she doesn't have a
grandfather.

13.68.

RUDOLPH
We could pretend I'm your grandfather –

13.69.

Albert and Bettina alone. Some time later.

ALBERT
We've got to do something –

BETTINA
But what?

ALBERT
That man has got to go.

BETTINA
Then throw him out.

ALBERT
I can't throw him out.

BETTINA
You said he's got to go. So go on then. Throw him out. Get on
with it.

13.70.

Albert looks at Bettina. For a long time.
He remembers an afternoon ten years ago in France, on the
Atlantic coast. Summer. The sun is already low, the waves
as high as houses. The red flag is flying and now, after work,
the lifeguards are out swimming with their surfboards. Their
heads and arms on the peaks of those glittering mountains of
water. Nothing can harm those men.

13.71.

Bettina tells the child: time for bed.
The child shouts: Noooo! Her mother says: Yes it is. Daddy
will read to you. The child: Noooo! Rudolph says: Young
lady! Tomorrow is going to be an exciting day.
Her mother says: clean your teeth and off to bed.

14.1.

In the child's bedroom. A lamp which projects stars onto the
ceiling in the darkness. Cuddly toys. Wooden toys. Marie has
a beautiful large room. Her father puts his daughter to bed.
He lies down next to her on top of the bed, she snuggles up to
him. Both watch the snow falling outside the window.
Both breathe easily.
The doorbell rings. The child wants to jump up. Her father
says: stay here.
The daughter asks her father: Who is it?
Bettina shouts from the entrance hall: I'll get it.
It is just after ten.
Bettina opens the front door.

14.2.

Bettina opens the door to the flat.
Outside the door stands a young woman.
– Hello, the young woman says to Bettina.
Bettina has seen the young woman once before at her
husband's publishers.
– Hello.
The young woman says: I'd like to talk to Albert –

14.3.

In the child's bedroom. The child in bed. Her father lies next
to her, he has taken off his shoes. The daughter asks:
– Daddy? Can God see through clouds?
He says: Yes.

14.4.

At the door to the flat. Bettina and the young woman.
The young woman says: I'd like to talk to Albert –
Bettina says: He – he's just putting our daughter to bed –
She shrugs her shoulders. She does not invite the young
woman in.
– Yes, I know, it's late, I – says the young woman. Her eye-
liner has run. She has been crying.

– I, I didn't want to disturb you – Could you give him
something for me?
– Yes, of course –

14.5.

In the child's bedroom:
– And does God sleep at night?
– No.
– Does he ever sleep?
– I don't know.
– Because he's got to sleep.
– Do you think so?
– Don't you? I think he sleeps sometimes. In winter, the girl
says.
– In winter? And what happens while he's asleep?
– Then people are alone.
Yes, her father thinks. People are alone.

14.6.

At the same time at the front door.
The young woman says: We, we work together and I forgot to
give him this –
Bettina says, I know, I know who you are – I saw you recently
at the publishers –
– Well then – the young woman gives Bettina an envelope –
here. Thanks. Merry Christmas.
Bettina says: You too.
The woman says: Thanks.
Bettina says: Don't mention it.

14.7.

In the child's bedroom: The child has fallen asleep. Albert
stays there for a few minutes, lying beside the little girl in the
dark. The stars on the ceiling. The restful breathing of the
child at his side.

10.15 p.m.
For a moment everything is fine just the way it is.

14.8.

In the kitchen. Corinna and Rudolph and Konrad.
Albert is still with the child, Bettina has been at the door for a
couple of minutes.

CORINNA
And all that goes unrecognized.
Nothing is recognized.
Old people are starving.
Who is going to look after me?

14.9.

Bettina comes back into the kitchen.
Corinna feels she has been caught out.

14.10.

CORINNA
Certainly not you.
At the end of the month there's nothing, nothing left.

BETTINA
Nice dress.

RUDOLPH
Yes, isn't it? That's what I said –

14.11.

Corinna knows what this intervention from her daughter implies.
She knows that it is not a compliment. She knows that her
daughter is trying to say that she is not telling the truth.

14.12.

CORINNA
It's second hand.

14.13.

Corinna lights a cigarette.

14.14.

CORINNA
New: but second hand. You have to look out for yourself. It
was less than half price. Less than a third.

BETTINA
You don't need to justify yourself.

14.15.

BETTINA lights a cigarette.
Corinna stands up, tense, and starts clearing up.

14.16.

CORINNA
Are you smoking again?

BETTINA
Hardly ever.

14.17.

Konrad laughs out loud. He takes Albert's reading glasses,
which have been left lying on the kitchen table, puts them on
and takes them off again. Konrad doesn't need reading glasses.
Finally he puts the glasses back down on the table.

14.18.

10.27 p.m.
Just before Albert is about to fall asleep himself, he has an idea
for his next book: *'Christmas in Auschwitz'.*
Albert stands up carefully.
He looks out of the window of the child's bedroom.
He sees the perfect blanket of snow in the light of the street
lamps. He remembers how magical nights like this were when
he was a child.
For a moment he thinks he can see Naomi in the snow down
in front of the building. She is standing in the street looking up
at the window but then suddenly she's gone. Nobody there.
He must have been mistaken.

14.19.

CORINNA
Give me one of those.

BETTINA
But you're already smoking –

14.20.

RUDOLPH laughs.

14.21.

RUDOLPH
It's true!

CORINNA
My feet still hurt. From the cold.

KONRAD
Was it that cold in the train?

CORINNA
Freezing. And I was in these shoes, I had the wrong shoes on,
who expects something like that to happen –

BETTINA
Mother, please leave everything where it is. We're still eating.
Just sit down –

14.22.

Bettina knows what her mother is like when she's nervous.
When she feels attacked. When it comes out that she has lied,
like just now, about the dress, which of course she didn't buy
second hand.
Bettina knows or can predict with almost absolute certainty
that her mother is going to break something in the next five
minutes.

14.23.

Albert picks up his shoes and slips out of the child's bedroom.

14.24.

In the kitchen. Corinna continues clearing up.

BETTINA
Mother, please leave everything where it is. We're still eating.
Just sit down –.

CORINNA
No, no, it's alright.

14.25.

Corinna wants to tidy the kitchen, she doesn't want to sit
down, but does it for her daughter's sake, though only half
does it: she half sits down on the kitchen table – a crack,
something breaks –

14.26.

Albert slips out of the child's bedroom and gently closes the
door. He walks down the corridor with his shoes in his hand.
Then he steps on a piece of broken glass. It is 10.30 p.m.

14.27.1.

> Flashback:
> It is 6.20 p.m.

14.27.2.

> BETTINA
> What was that?
> No answer.

> ALBERT
> What was that?

14.28.

> A crack, something smashes –

14.29.

> CORINNA
> Oh, oh, oh no.

> BETTINA
> What, what's happened?

> CORINNA
> I didn't mean to, I really didn't mean to do that –

> BETTINA
> What, what is it –

14.30.

> Corinna has sat on Albert's reading glasses which were lying
> on the kitchen table.

14.31.

> BETTINA
> Never mind –

> CORINNA
> But I am really so very –

14.32.

> Blood. Blood on the floor in the entrance hall. Blood on the
> floor in the bathroom. Albert's foot is bleeding.
> Albert in the bathroom, his bleeding foot on the edge of the
> bath, Albert looks for a plaster and finds one. His phone rings.
> Before he can answer it, Bettina comes into the bathroom.

14.33.

BETTINA
My mother's just sat on your reading glasses –

ALBERT in a rough voice.
What?

BETTINA
She sat on your glasses –

ALBERT
But how – how am I supposed –

14.34.

It slowly becomes clear to him what this means.

14.35.

ALBERT
How am I going to –

BETTINA
It just happened –

ALBERT
How can that just happen –

BETTINA
It just did.

ALBERT
But without any glasses I can't –

15.1.

Some time later in the living room. Corinna, Rudolph and Konrad on the sofa and comfy chairs. Bettina starts decorating the Christmas tree. Albert limps into the room and sits down in a chair.

15.2.

CORINNA
I am so very sorry, really –

ALBERT slightly dazed.
You don't have to apologize –

CORINNA
But you have to be able to read –

ALBERT
In three days when the shops are open again –

CORINNA
I don't know, it's best if I leave –

ALBERT
No, no, that's not going to change anything –

CORINNA
Or you could try my reading glasses for the time being, then
I won't be able to read anything but in my case that's not so
important – here, please, take mine –

RUDOLPH
Or you can take mine, I've got some too –

ALBERT
No, no –

15.3.

A little earlier. In the bathroom. Bettina sees Albert's bleeding
foot with the plaster, but says nothing.
Instead she gives Albert the envelope.

15.4.

BETTINA
Here –

ALBERT
What's that?

BETTINA
Someone left it for you.

ALBERT
What? When?

BETTINA
Just now.

ALBERT
Who?

BETTINA
A young woman. From the publishers.

ALBERT
Oh yes –

15.5.

Bettina looks at him quickly and goes back into the kitchen.
Albert stays alone in the bathroom. He opens the envelope. It
contains some banknotes and a letter.
He tries to read the letter but he can't read it without his
reading glasses.

15.6.

Music.
10.50 p.m. in the living room. Bettina decorating the
Christmas tree. Konrad helping her.
Rudolph and Corinna are drinking red wine. Konrad is also
drinking red wine, although he's decorating the Christmas tree
at the same time. Albert does not know what to do. He would
like to read the letter but he can't without reading glasses.

15.7.

10.55 p.m. Rudolph at the piano.
Bach, Prelude 16 in G minor from the Well-Tempered Clavier
Book 1.

15.8.

11p.m.

15.9.

RUDOLPH
There just aren't any Jewish composers, well I can't think of
any –
Strictly speaking there aren't even any Catholic composers
worth taking seriously –

ALBERT
Mendelssohn, Mahler, Weill –

KONRAD
Oh – And what about Mozart –

15.10.

Suddenly his heart is racing again, he's sweating, he has an
attack of dizziness.
Albert looks at his watch.

11.03 p.m.

15.11.

Ten minutes later.
11.13 p.m.
The Christmas tree looks more and more beautiful.

15.12.

CORINNA
I would have liked to have been something else – I would
have liked to learn an instrument, I would have liked to go to
university, like my daughter, like you, but you know, in our
family that wasn't to be taken for granted – my father – they
were different times –

RUDOLPH
But you are something –

CORINNA
Yees, but –

RUDOLPH
No, you're something wonderful –

CORINNA
Yes?

RUDOLPH
You're a mother. You are a grandmother. You have achieved
a lot. You've brought a healthy daughter into the world and
that daughter has brought a healthy child into the world who's
as quick as lightning. You've made your contribution and that
must be recognized. Must it not?

15.13.

RUDOLPH looks around the group.

15.14.

11.16 p.m.

15.15.

RUDOLPH
That must be recognized and a society which does not
recognize this is –

15.16.

He pauses. Rudolph takes Corinna's hand. A look from
mother to daughter.

15.17.

RUDOLPH
You can be proud. No! You must be proud.

CORINNA
"Proud" – that's another of those words which is completely
out of fashion. "Proud" and "chivalry". And "decency."

15.18.

It is 11.20 p.m.
Rudolph discovers Bettina's films lying on the occasional
table.

15.19.

RUDOLPH
Are those your films?
How interesting…

BETTINA
Yes, they're some of my –

15.20.

The titles of the films in Rudolph's hand:
'Robert and I'.
'One Week in Germany'.
'Life would not be Life'.
Rudolph's eyes fall on Konrad's paintbrush, lying next to her
films on the table.
Bettina would like to carry on talking about her films –

15.21.

RUDOLPH
And that? How beautiful!

ALBERT
What?

BETTINA
Those – those are my –

RUDOLPH
Oh, look –

CORINNA
Yes –

RUDOLPH
Look –

15.22.

He holds up the paintbrush.

15.23.

RUDOLPH
How beautiful –

15.24.

Konrad's face. He is beaming. His hungover, unshaven face is suddenly beaming, his tired eyes have changed. He does not know what is coming but he has the feeling that something special is about to happen, that he is on the verge of a special moment in his life. Of a turning point.

15.25.

RUDOLPH takes his time.
How beautiful. Isn't it?

15.26.

Corinna does not understand what he means but she says "Yes."

15.27.

CORINNA
Yes.

15.28.

This yes resonates with fascination, devotion, enthusiasm and amazement.

15.29.

RUDOLPH
What do you see?

15.30.

Corinna wants to say something but she does not know what, so she just says "Well, well."

15.31.

CORINNA
Well, well –

RUDOLPH
What do you see?

ALBERT
Well – I – I see a paintbrush.

15.32.

Konrad laughs. Bettina laughs too.

15.33.

RUDOLPH
A paintbrush!
But with this –
with this one cannot only paint a picture, your friend Konrad knows what I am talking about. With this –

15.34.

Rudolph keeps holding up the paintbrush –

15.35.

RUDOLPH
With this one can create a world.

15.36.

11.25 p.m.

15.37.

RUDOLPH
A new world which will endure for ever.
A picture, a picture is closer to people than a photograph which is nothing but the reproduction or the deformation of the present, but a picture, is this not right, Konrad, do correct me on this, a picture opens hearts and it opens eyes – if it is truly art.
Because this here –

15.38.

He continues to hold up the paintbrush.

15.39.

RUDOLPH
This here – this here – is a torch!

15.40.

Bettina laughs and continues to decorate the tree.

15.41.

Thirty minutes later.
Just before midnight.

15.42.

RUDOLPH
I think we have to be prepared to question everything.
Everything.

CORINNA
Mmmh.

ALBERT
Yes, but what does that mean –

RUDOLPH
Everything is exploding. We are drifting further and further
apart.
And no one can find the way back.
We have to find the way to a place where the community is
still a community. The path to unity.

15.43.

Corinna nods.

15.44.

RUDOLPH
It's as if we are all trapped in a set pattern. We go left, right,
straight ahead, as if we can only move on existing tracks.

KONRAD
That's right.

RUDOLPH
We need new thinking.

Completely new.
We have to start playing the music of the cosmos once again.
Let's join together.
Come together in one big sound.
Together we are strong.

15.45.

Rudolph lays his hand on Konrad's shoulder.

15.46.

RUDOLPH
And it is the torch which leads us, which brings light into the darkness.

15.47.

Corinna applauds.

15.48.

12.05 a.m. Albert and Bettina briefly alone in the kitchen.

ALBERT
The things he's saying –

BETTINA
At least he's not boring –

15.49.

12.08 a.m.
In the living room.
Konrad, Rudolph, Bettina, Corinna and Albert.

RUDOLPH
You have 12 square metres of canvas to fill, let's say 12 square metres, 4 metres by 3, for example, we won't start by talking about a whole wall of a building, or a ceiling the size of the Sistine Chapel, but still – you know, 12 square metres is a world, a universe –

KONRAD
I'd like a drop more wine.

RUDOLPH
We are called upon to make the world richer, brighter – art in particular –

ALBERT
Excuse me, a picture is a picture and not a candle –

CORINNA
Torch –

KONRAD
No, no, questioning the relevance of art is justified –

ALBERT
But who gets to say what's relevant and what isn't –

KONRAD
Individualism is no more than hollow euphoria –

ALBERT
Only because you've drunk too much –

KONRAD
We hide away in our pain and our desires and we end up
crawling around on the earth in the dark when we could be
flying –

RUDOLPH
The truth is radiant.

ALBERT
I don't think the truth is radiant at all.
There is no truth.

KONRAD
Of course there's truth.

RUDOLPH
Truth – life, death, the sun – those are truths –

ALBERT
Do you know how far away the sun is from us?

RUDOLPH
And that makes the struggle so much more important – the
struggle –

CORINNA tipsy:
The truth of chivalrous battle.

15.50.

Rudolph places his hand on his girlfriend's hand.

15.51.

ALBERT
The struggle –

KONRAD
The struggle –

RUDOLPH
The struggle –
The idea.

ALBERT
The idea – the idea of what?

RUDOLPH laughs.
The idea of beauty –

15.52.

Albert feels for the pills in his trouser pocket and takes one of them, which he swallows with a gulp of red wine. It is one of the white ones.
Bettina has been watching her husband. She knows what reaching into his trouser pocket for pills means.
12.12 a.m.

15.53.

BETTINA
Is everything alright?

ALBERT
Hm? Yeah, yeah –

15.54.

Albert heads into the bathroom.

15.55.

CORINNA to Bettina, while Albert has still not quite left the room.
Well – well he keeps on –

16.1.

Albert in the bathroom. He opens the mirrored cabinet. He takes some pills out of the cabinet. These pills are green.
He closes the mirrored cabinet again. His eyes are suddenly transfixed.

16.2.

ALBERT
How did you find me?

RUDOLPH
What do you mean find?
She invited me –

ALBERT
I thought they'd hanged you.

RUDOLPH
Hanged? Me? Why?

ALBERT
Because you –

RUDOLPH laughs.
No, no, oh no –

ALBERT
But you're the butcher of –

RUDOLPH
The butcher, what kind of butcher –

16.3.

CORINNA kisses Rudolph.

16.4.

CORINNA
Just don't listen.

ALBERT
You are the butcher of –

RUDOLPH
The doctor – not the butcher –

ALBERT to Bettina.
I thought he was dead – and what have I got to do with him –
what can I do about it – That man is a monster!

BETTINA
What?

ALBERT whispers.
That man is a monster.
We've got to kill him.

CORINNA
You're up to something.
I can see that about you.
You're not going to destroy my future, you've destroyed
enough already.

ALBERT
I thought you were dead –
You've been dead for years!

16.5.

Rudolph makes a good-natured snapping sound with his
tongue.

16.6.

RUDOLPH
Dead? Well –

16.7.

RUDOLPH laughs –

16.8.

RUDOLPH
I'd say I'm not quite dead, not quite. The old are tougher than
many people think. I was afraid you were going to leave me
standing in the hallway.
Merry Christmas.

17.1

Some time later in the living room. Albert returns.

17.2.

RUDOLPH
There you are –

17.3.

He drinks some wine.
Bettina has almost finished decorating the tree, but
keeps changing small details. The antique Christmas tree
decorations. Things she has made herself.
The candles.
Albert is rather woozy, but tries not to show it.

17.4.1.

RUDOLPH
The idea of beauty serves mankind, does it not?
Is that not right?
The idea of beauty serves mankind –

17.4.2.

He drinks some more wine. He seems to have completed his thought, but then carries on with it.

17.4.3.

RUDOLPH
So someone who does not serve that idea is not serving mankind either. Is he?

17.4.4.

Albert drinks some wine which goes down the wrong way.

17.4.5.

RUDOLPH
And anyone who does not serve mankind,
betrays the species.
Anyone who betrays the species does not deserve to be part of that species.

17.4.6.

Albert drinks some wine which goes down the wrong way, coughs, but tries to suppress the cough.

17.4.7.

RUDOLPH
Anyone who betrays the species is not human.
He might be human in a biological sense perhaps, but in actual fact he is no longer part of mankind –

17.5.

Bettina decorating the tree.

17.6.

RUDOLPH
He is something similar to a human, a body, an organism, an animal – and yes, humans have the right to kill that animal just as that animal kills humans, and that, that is the struggle.

KONRAD
No.

17.7.

Rudolph taken aback. Bettina stops what she's doing.

17.8.

RUDOLPH
No?

KONRAD
Mankind does not have the right.

RUDOLPH
Young man –

KONRAD
Mankind does not have the right.
It is its duty.
It is its duty.

17.9.

12.24 a.m.

KONRAD gets up and goes into the kitchen. He seems to open a drawer there and be looking for something. He returns with a large knife.

17.10.

ALBERT
What are you doing? What are you doing?

KONRAD
Don't you know – you must see –
This is long overdue.

17.11.

Holding the knife, Konrad goes up to the large oil painting and slashes it to pieces.

17.12.

BETTINA
Konrad –

KONRAD
This is not art.

This is not the art we will take with us into the future. No.

17.13.

He continues to destroy the picture which he himself painted.

17.14.

ALBERT
Hey –

17.15.

Bettina lays her hand on Konrad's hand holding the knife.

17.16.

BETTINA
Konrad –

17.17.

Konrad kisses Bettina on the mouth.

17.18.

ALBERT
What's going on now?

KONRAD
It was time.

ALBERT
Watch you don't hurt yourself –

CORINNA
Well, that –

17.19.

Corinna looks at Rudolph.

17.20.

RUDOLPH
Let's put everything behind us.

KONRAD
All that is merely the illustration of an aimless search – but now:

17.21.

Konrad lays special emphasis on these words:

17.22.

KONRAD
From now on:

BETTINA
Konrad –

17.23.

He stops. He can see a large new picture with his inner eye – :

17.24.

ALBERT
A pity about that canvas. I think I lent you the money for that canvas.

17.25.

In the picture in Konrad's head: people joining together, moving towards the horizon.

17.26.

BETTINA quietly.
What are you doing? Have you had too much to drink?

17.27.

Konrad looks at her for a long time. He takes her hand.

KONRAD
No.
Too little.

ALBERT
I think you've had too much.

17.28.

Chopin. Nocturne.
It snows and snows in the night beyond the large windows of this old apartment. Corinna, laughing, shakes her head.
Rudolph puts his arm around her shoulders.
Konrad gesticulates to explain something, his eyes shining.
Bettina carries on decorating the tree.
The large oil painting, hanging in tatters on the wall.
Albert rubs his eyes. The pills in his hands.
Rudolph opens his suitcase and takes out a white plastic bag.
In the bag: a bottle.

Bettina climbs onto a chair next to the tree.
Rudolph takes the cork out of the bottle.
Corinna fetches some small glasses.
Bettina places the evening star on top of the Christmas tree.
She almost falls off her chair, but Konrad catches her.
Rudolph pours a clear liquid into the small glasses.
Corinna holds her glass in her hand, with a questioning and
curious look. Konrad holds his glass in his hand and can
hardly wait to drink it. Bettina with a glass. Albert does not
touch the glass in front of him.
Rudolph says something but music covers the scene.

17.29.

The music stops.

RUDOLPH
Dear friends – well, I don't know, on such a special night –
here I am under your roof –

17.30.

The slashed painting.

17.31.

CORINNA
Yes –

RUDOLPH
And I'm just the guest
but I am the oldest –
shall we drink to our friendship?

17.32.

12.33 a.m. Albert wants to say something –

17.33.

CORINNA
Well, well, – you're very welcome, more than welcome –

ALBERT
That depends –

BETTINA amused.
Well I –

RUDOLPH
Gudrun –

Bettina –
Albert –
Konrad –
Do you see this?

17.34.

He holds a glass and the bottle in his hand. Konrad with the
knife.

17.35.

RUDOLPH
I – I brought something with me, something special – Albert,
Bettina –
Gudrun –

17.35.

Rudolph raises the bottle in the air. He pauses for a long time.

17.36.

RUDOLPH
Whoever drinks this water will live for ever.
No! Not quite.
But still!
Whoever drinks this water, will live for a thousand years.

CORINNA
A thousand years?

ALBERT
Is that all?

17.37.

Corinna looks at the glass in fascination.

17.38.

CORINNA
A thousand years?

ALBERT
Is that all?

RUDOLPH
You don't have to believe it but it would be nice if we had
something which we could believe in –

ALBERT
Belief, well, if it's belief we're talking about –

KONRAD
Belief, yes!

ALBERT
Then I can believe in eternal life just as well without it –

KONRAD laughs dirtily –
In the land of forgetfulness, in paradise –

ALBERT
Or in hell –

CORINNA has not been listening.
Oh how nice.

RUDOLPH
It looks like water but it is the distilled essence of life –

BETTINA
What's that?

RUDOLPH
This – this is – it's a legacy.
A task.
A mystery.

17.39.

Corinna picks up the bottle and looks at it.

17.40.

RUDOLPH
Careful –

BETTINA
Mother –

RUDOLPH
No, no, please – leave her, it's alright, everything is alright –

17.41.

Rudolph raises his glass.

17.42.

RUDOLPH
Gudrun –

ALBERT
Corinna –

RUDOLPH
A thousand years.

CORINNA looks at him seriously.
A thousand years, Rudolph.

17.43.

Corinna drinks. The glass at her mouth.

17.44.

CORINNA with pleasure.
Aaaah.

17.45.

Rudolph takes hold of her hand and does not let go.

17.46.

RUDOLPH
A thousand years.

17.47.

There is a pause. Konrad reaches for his glass.

17.48.

KONRAD
I'm in.

17.49.

He empties his glass.

17.50.

KONRAD
Thank you.

17.51.

Bettina hesitates, but then drinks all of her glass.

17.52.

Albert sips at his glass –
But this – this is just water –

17.53.

> The script is missing something, the producer had said. "The material is interesting, though what does interesting mean, but it lacks – 'blood'".
> "Blood?" Bettina had asked.

17.54.

> 12.39 a.m. Konrad suddenly throws his glass behind him.

17.55.

RUDOLPH
But, but – what are you doing?

KONRAD
What's the matter? Are we celebrating or aren't we? The solstice.

17.56.

> 12.42 a.m.

17.57.

RUDOLPH
We have to stop this mixing.
This contamination.
We had a garden and then the aphids came.
"The canker galls the infants of the spring
Too oft before their buttons be disclosed.
And in the morn and liquid dew of youth
Contagious blastments are most imminent."
Nature seeks its own order.
And order consists of boundaries.
Boundaries exist. That is the law of nature.
Purity, clarity. Boundaries are boundaries. Cultures are cultures, that's the way it is, that's how it always was. Beware of mixing.
Beware of aphids.

17.58.

> Corinna smiles knowingly.
> Rudolph is pleased with this smile.

17.59.

RUDOLPH laughs.
But –

17.60.

He laughs.

17.61.

RUDOLPH
But Konrad, you, you know where the old masters got their purple pigment from: from aphids.
That is the order of nature, the lower serves the higher. It's always been like that –

17.62.

Rudolph laughs.
Konrad stares into emptiness. Hollow.

17.63.

KONRAD
Yes, that's how it is. Legions of aphids.

17.64.

12.44 a.m.

RUDOLPH
Paris, Moscow –

18.1.

It is 12.45 a.m.

RUDOLPH
Suffering.
All the greats have suffered. The greats are willing to sacrifice themselves.

18.2.

12.46 a.m.

18.3.

RUDOLPH
Who is bothered about the curve or the breadth of a nose, those are all mistakes or let's say, misjudgements, though –

18.4.

Albert tries to stand up.

18.5.

RUDOLPH
Though – so many misjudgements nevertheless do lead to
something, they reach what one could call the right conclusion
from the wrong hypothesis, don't they:
just as many wrong conclusions are drawn from the right
hypotheses, –

18.6.

Albert tries to stand up. He can tell that he should not stand
up but he stands up regardless. Suddenly everything before
his eyes goes black, his knees give way, he falls to the floor but
gets back up again straight away.

18.7.

KONRAD
Hey –

BETTINA
Is everything –

KONRAD
Hey –

CORINNA
Oh –

RUDOLPH
But, but –

BETTINA
Is everything alright?

RUDOLPH
You'd be better off –

18.8.

Albert has trouble catching his breath but is then loud.

18.9.

ALBERT
You – you are going to leave my house now!

CORINNA
What?

ALBERT
Out!

RUDOLPH
Me –

ALBERT
You leave – my house – now!

CORINNA
Well – really ! What a –

ALBERT
That's enough!

RUDOLPH
I don't know what I can say–

ALBERT
That's enough!

BETTINA
Albert –

ALBERT
You go on and on talking and it's all complete –

CORINNA
If he goes, then I'm going too!

KONRAD
Look, Albert –

RUDOLPH
Corinna, please – Albert, I don't know how I, if I – if in any
conceivable way I can have – and you don't seem to be in
such a good way right now, but that, that was not –

BETTINA
Albert, darling, what's the –

ALBERT
But what – what?

18.10.

Albert sees a full wine glass in front of him. He looks into
Rudolph's face.
Rudolph thinks: why is he looking at me like that?

18.11.

Albert throws the wine in Rudolph's face. Slow motion. The wine in the air.
The wine in Rudolph's face.

18.12.

CORINNA
Oh! Oh! Oh!

BETTINA
Albert...

18.13.

Rudolph would like to punch the man who has just thrown wine in his face but he quashes this impulse.

18.14.

RUDOLPH
Now – now –

18.15.

He looks around for something to dry his face with and eventually pulls an old fashioned gentleman's handkerchief out of his pocket. He clears his throat. He controls himself.

18.16.

RUDOLPH
Now – it is time to leave.

ALBERT
I think so too.

RUDOLPH
I am leaving. I came as a guest, you accepted me into your home and now it seems I am no longer welcome.

18.17.

Corinna wants to take his hand.

18.18.

RUDOLPH
So I shall go. Thank you, Bettina.
And you, Albert.
Give me your hand.

Let's just forget this –
No?
As you wish. People always meet twice and the second time is
very different.

CORINNA
Why did you do that?

ALBERT
It was the right conclusion from the right hypothesis.

BETTINA
This is my mother.

ALBERT
Yes, I know she's your mother.

BETTINA
But you don't care.

ALBERT
No, no. On the contrary. Mothers are the most important
thing in life. I wish I still had a mother.

BETTINA
Your mother was never interested in you.
Your mother was a cruel woman.
My mother is just lonely.
And now she's met someone new.
You create nothing but animosity.
You exclude her.

18.19.

Rudolph suddenly loses control. He pulls his arm back ready
to slap.

18.20.

RUDOLPH shouts.
Who do you actually think you –, you filthy Jew –

19.1.

It is 12.46 a.m.
The child wakes up. She can hear the voices of the adults in
the living room.
Rudolph says: "Though – so many misjudgements
nevertheless do lead to something, they reach what one could
call the right conclusion from the wrong hypothesis, don't

125

they: just as many wrong conclusions are drawn from the right hypotheses."

The girl slips out of bed and sneaks along the corridor.

19.2.

KONRAD
Hey –

BETTINA
Is everything –

KONRAD
Hey –

CORINNA
Oh –

RUDOLPH
But, but –

BETTINA
Is everything alright?

RUDOLPH
You'd be better off –

CORINNA
Perhaps you should lie down.

19.3.

Albert is so dizzy he can hardly hear what she's saying to him, his ears are full of noise.

Rudolph feels Albert's pulse.

19.4.

CORINNA
You really should lie down.

RUDOLPH
Is that better?

KONRAD
Hey!

ALBERT
What?

KONRAD
You were out of it for a while –

ALBERT
What? Me? Out of it?

KONRAD
Yes, out of it. You were totally out of it for a while –
It was quite scary –

ALBERT
When?

BETTINA
Do you need a doctor?

CORINNA
Rudolph is a doctor –

KONRAD
You just keeled over.

ALBERT
I'm not –

BETTINA
Should we call your doctor –

RUDOLPH
I don't think that's necessary – I'm –

19.5.

Albert's wide open eyes.
The slashed, ruined picture on the wall.
Rudolph's shirt, the collar without red wine stains.
No red wine in Rudolph's face.
Rudolph, continuing to take Albert's pulse. Bettina, Corinna
and Konrad around Albert, worrying.
Albert tries to catch Bettina's eye and can't.

19.6.

ALBERT
I – didn't I just, but I –

BETTINA
What?

CORINNA
He's always ill at Christmas, and always when there are
visitors –

RUDOLPH
You work too hard. You do work too hard – and these tablets, what kind of tablets are they, that you've –

19.7.

Marie, his daughter, is standing in the doorway wearing a beautiful long nightie. The child can see that her father seems to be in a bad way. The child says: Daddy? Daddy? Are you poorly?

19.8.

ALBERT
What? Aren't you in bed?
No, no –

BETTINA
Daddy just felt a bit dizzy for a while.

ALBERT
Why aren't you in bed – go back to bed –

19.9.

Dizzy, the girl asks, why?
The girl sees the Christmas tree with all its decorations.
She asks: Is it Christmas now?
– Yes, her grandmother says, today is Christmas.
– Really?
The girl is thrilled.
The girl looks for and finds matches.
She climbs onto a chair and starts lighting the candles on the Christmas tree, one after another.
The child's beautiful, shining face.
The burning match.
The burning candles.
Look, Daddy!
How beautiful. Are you feeling better?

19.10.

The burning candles.
Albert's phone makes a noise.

19.11.

BETTINA
How beautiful.

How beautiful. Marie. Come here.

19.12.

She pulls the child to her.

19.13.

BETTINA
Turn the light off, Konrad –

19.14.

Konrad turns off the light. Darkness. Only the burning candles
on the Christmas tree.

19.15.

CORINNA
Ooooh –

19.16.

The child on her mother's lap. Corinna next to Rudolph, hand
in hand. Konrad sits down and smiles at Bettina.
Albert has the feeling he can't breathe.

19.17.

ALBERT quietly.
I – I'm not like you think, I just can't –

BETTINA smiles.
Neither am I. I'm not like you think either.

19.18.

A moment of silence. Rudolph clears his throat and stands up.

19.19.

RUDOLPH
May I –

19.20.

Rudolph sits down at the piano.
He plays Bach, Prelude No. 1 in C major.
The Well-Tempered Clavier Book 1.
A cold winter night.

It continues to snow outside the large windows of the apartment.
The Christmas tree.
The bright flames of the candles.
The focus softens.
Slow dissolve.
The Well-Tempered Clavier, Prelude No. 8 in E-flat minor, BWV 853.
Credits.
The End.